Food With Friends

Background credit: FreePik

Food With Friends

Food With Friends

Grain-Free, Lactose-Free, and Refined-Sugar-Free

Appetizers, Breads, Tapas, Group Meals, Desserts & More!

Share Your Hospitality & Food with Friends & Family!

Robin S. Cox

Design and Photographs by Robin S. Cox

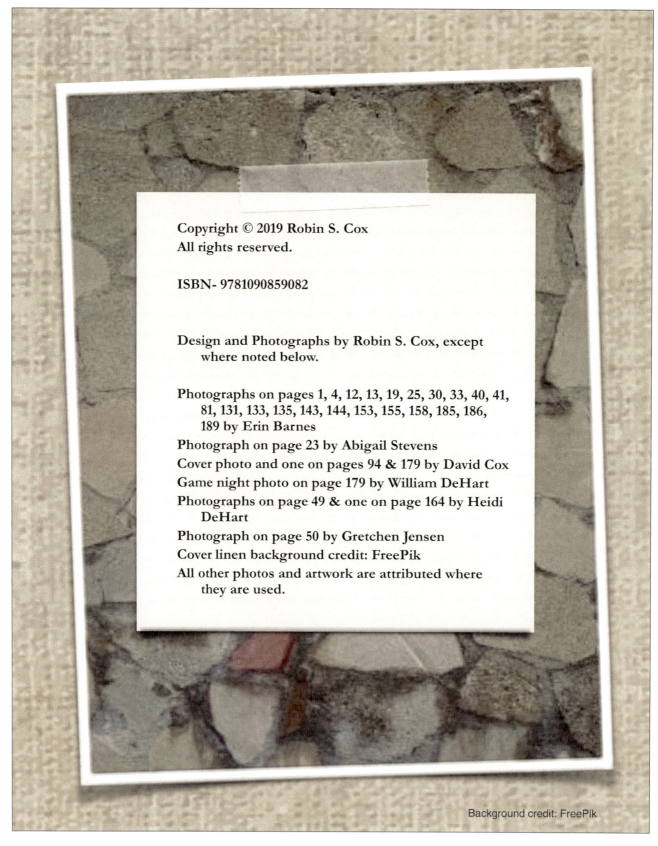

Copyright © 2019 Robin S. Cox
All rights reserved.

ISBN- 9781090859082

Design and Photographs by Robin S. Cox, except where noted below.

Photographs on pages 1, 4, 12, 13, 19, 25, 30, 33, 40, 41, 81, 131, 133, 135, 143, 144, 153, 155, 158, 185, 186, 189 by Erin Barnes
Photograph on page 23 by Abigail Stevens
Cover photo and one on pages 94 & 179 by David Cox
Game night photo on page 179 by William DeHart
Photographs on page 49 & one on page 164 by Heidi DeHart
Photograph on page 50 by Gretchen Jensen
Cover linen background credit: FreePik
All other photos and artwork are attributed where they are used.

Background credit: FreePik

Dedication

To Jim Barnes, my son-in-law,
Erin's husband, and
creator of the very popular "Jim's Fluffy Pancakes!"

Background credit: FreePik

Food With Friends

Background credit: FreePik

Contents

Thank You's, 4

Introduction, 6

What Makes It "Legal?", 11

Appetizers & Drinks, 15

Breads & Muffins, 35

Group Meals, 57

Main Dish Tapas (Small Plates), 97

Side Dish Tapas (Small Plates), 117

Desserts, 125

Salsas, Dips & Sauces, 163

Recipe Index, 180

Bonus Dessert Section, 184

Acknowledgements

I'm grateful to so many people for their help, tangible and intangible, in the creation of this new cookbook which provides the Specific Carbohydrate Diet community with creative and fun recipes to share with friends, and shares some thoughts on hospitality. I'll just list people as they come to mind. Thanks to…

• The people in the SCD community, some of whom we met at the SCDROCKS conference, who inspire me as I create this cookbook. I'd like you to have more fun with your food!

• A high school English teacher from Pittsburg, Pennsylvania, who sat at our table during the SCDROCKS conference. I got to see his delighted face filled with anticipation as he ordered *The Flavor First Cookbook* online to help him and his wife cook better meals, and this memory made me think of all the other people who have enjoyed my first effort, and made me feel it would be worthwhile to create another cookbook.

• The supportive friends who have attended my taster's meals to evaluate recipes and offer helpful critique while building friendships among ourselves. You know who you are!

• Diane Fillmore, who is a friend, book editor, and publisher, and greatly encouraged my efforts. She gave me the idea of including the group meals section as she has enjoyed many group meals at our home and seen how different diets have been "effortlessly" accommodated.

• The many thousands of visitors to NoMoreCrohns.com who have loved many of these recipes in their downloadable form and can now have them in convenient book form.

• ReluctantEntertainer, whose blog is an inspiration to me.

• My family members, who continue to encourage and support me in all my endeavors.

• You, who purchased this book! I hope it enriches your life and your table.

Digging Into Taco Salads at a Tasters' Lunch

Background credit: FreePik

Introduction

See p. 168

What do you think of when I say "Food With Friends?" Does it give you a little jolt of happiness? Does it scare you? Have you felt that maybe it's not possible anymore because of your diet? For me, those three words make me happy! I love getting together with friends and family to share moments of laughter, tasting, chatting, listening, and savoring. And it's all still possible with your diet, which after all, is fresh, beautiful, normal food with some things eliminated for your health.

Being on the Specific Carbohydrate Diet doesn't need to stop you from sharing your life, your food, and your hospitality with others. It's been such a personal experience pulling this cookbook together and thinking of how it might inspire you to ease back into life because of the second chance you've been given through diet. When we share food we can provide items for everyone, then enjoy what works for us! It's the intangibles we remember later that make us say, "wasn't that a great evening?"

One of my favorite things about entertaining is seeing guests relax, enjoy the food, laugh, maybe make a new friend, and feel refreshed. We listen to one another, ask questions that bring out interesting ideas, experiences, and abilities, or we just catch up. One group meal I'll always remember is when one friend started sharing about meeting her birth family for the first time! We were all on the edges of our seats and really shared her joy in finding this new dimension in her life.

When was the last time you intentionally invited a person, or maybe a few people that you wanted to get to know better, over for a snack or a meal? Eating in restaurants is more common these days, but I feel that hospitality at home is a beautiful thing that draws people together and touches our hearts. When we've been in someone's kitchen, we know them a little better! This book is designed to inspire you to jump in and invite friends over for food! Opening up our lives to each other changes us for the better, so why not start here, start now? Let's do it.

Sincerely,

Robin Cox

P.S. I'm very excited to share a few brand new bread recipes that you'll only find here! I hope you love them! ♡ Robin

What Makes It "Legal?"

In presenting each recipe, I've tried to explain it in such a way that anyone could make it and be sure it will turn out to be safe for a person on the Specific Carbohydrate Diet (SCD) to eat. All recipes are also automatically gluten-free, lactose-free, grain-free and refined-sugar free, but my daughter Erin is following the SCD and has experienced a dramatic remission of her Crohn's Disease through diet since 2001, so that is my emphasis. I'd like you to be confident as you cook for yourself or someone you love. If you are following the diet to help relieve serious medical problems it's always safest to eat homemade food.

In many of the following recipes there is at least one ingredient that needs to be *"legal,"* such as "butter*." In this section I'd like to explain what that item will look like if it's *"legal."* It means that it contains only items that are safe for a person on the SCD to eat. Items that are *"illegal"* contain long-chain carbohydrates, so items that are *"legal"* are free of even a trace of long-chain carbs and contain either no carbs or only short-chain carbs. To be sure a prepared item is compatible with the SCD, obtain a written statement from the company to verify whether the product has any trace illegal ingredients that are not listed on the label. Companies can change their formulas, so if symptoms reoccur, it may be because a safe product has changed.

I'll list the items that appear in our recipes in alphabetical order, with a brief explanation of what to look for. I want to also point you to the very helpful Specific Carbohydrate Diet "legal-illegal" list, presented on the official website for *Breaking the Vicious Cycle* and the Specific Carbohydrate Diet, which you'll find at http://www.breakingtheviciouscycle.info/legal/listing/.

See p. 154

Almond Butter: See Nut Butters.

Almond Extract: Water, alcohol and oil of bitter almond (no sugars added)

Almond Milk: May be tried after being on the diet for six months. We use Malk, which contains only almonds, salt and water.

Apple cider: Apple cider is legal because it is made from only apples whereas apple juice may have had sugars added during processing.

Artichoke Hearts: Make sure artichoke hearts are frozen or canned in water with no additives.

Bananas, speckled: Bananas need to be speckled because at that point the long-chain carbs are gone.

Blue Cheese: See Cheeses. Blue cheese is aged for about 2 months.

Broth: Broth should be homemade because purchased broths are usually made with potatoes or other illegal root vegetables. See p. 11 for a wonderful chicken broth recipe you can make and freeze. Whenever you cook a chicken, save and freeze the cooking liquid for later.

Butter: Real butter is a legal fat. No other margarine or butter substitute product may be substituted for real butter.

Canned meats (tuna, salmon, or chicken): If you are new to the diet use freshly cooked meats. Erin now successfully uses canned meats that are only canned in water or oil and salt, *not* with added ingredients such as broth, modified food starch, or natural flavors.

Coconut milk: The can should contain coconut milk, water, and possibly a preservative. It should *not* contain guar gum, cellulose, polysorbate, dried cane syrup, natural flavors, carrageenan, etc. Wait until you've been on the diet for six months before trying coconut products.

Cheeses, pre-grated: Pre-grated cheeses contain illegal starches to keep them from clumping, so we always grate our own.

Cheeses: Do they have lactose? In cheeses aged at least 30 days, the lactose has been digested away in the aging process, so these cheeses are legal.

Curry Powder: Curry powder is actually a combination of many spices and when these are combined commercially they add an anti-caking agent to the mixture, which is *not* legal. Use our recipe on p. 74, using individual spices, to make a little jar of your own curry powder.

See p. 132

Green chiles, diced: Page 62 tells how to roast your own Anaheim chiles. Erin now also uses canned chiles which contain diced green chiles, salt, citric acid, and a trace of calcium chloride. They *cannot* contain modified food starch, soy products, sugar, natural flavors, powdered spices, etc.

Granulated Garlic: Made from just dried garlic that has been granulated, we have researched the product from Costco and found it to contain nothing but garlic.

Granulated Onion: Made from just dried onion that has been granulated, we have researched the product from Costco and found it to contain nothing but onion.

Ground Dried Chiles: Just dried chili peppers that are ground with nothing added. We have used Tampico brand.

Hot pepper sauce: The original red Tabasco labeled "McIlhenny Company Tabasco Brand Pepper Sauce" which contains vinegar, red pepper, and salt, is the only compliant hot sauce we know of.

Mayonnaise: Erin loves to make her own from our simple recipe on page 176. It's the best way to make sure it's SCD legal.

Mustard, prepared: Regular yellow prepared mustard with only vinegar, mustard seed, salt, turmeric, and individual spices is legal. We have found that store brands are more likely to be legal and French's is *not* legal because it contains natural flavors (usually sugar) and garlic powder (the *powder* is the problem - that will be a starch). Specialty mustards may contain wheat, sugar, soy or other illegal items, so check carefully.

Navy beans: Navy beans are a type of bean listed as legal in the book *Breaking the Vicious Cycle*. You may try to introduce them to your diet after symptoms have improved substantially. You need to start with dried beans, soak them for 10-14 hours, drain and cook according to package directions. See our recipe on page 13.

Nut Butters: In cashew butter, almond butter, or peanut butter, make sure it's just the nuts and salt. It's also fine to have added palm fruit oil, which acts as a stabilizer in some brands.

Oil in a spray can: Put your own oil in a Misto sprayer. In the purchased canned sprays, the propellants contain illegals.

Olives: Olives are legal as long as they don't contain illegal ingredients such as sugars, lactic acid, or guar gum, etc.

Peanut butter: See Nut Butters.

Pickles: Dill pickles are legal if they don't contain any added sugars or other illegal ingredients. Other types of pickles contain sugar. If you want pickle relish, you can dice legal dill pickles and add honey to taste. We use Bubbies pickles with only legal ingredients.

See p. 146

Pickle juice: The juice from legal dill pickles (See Pickles).

Pimento: Pimento is roasted red bell pepper, so you can make your own (see p. 45), or if the jar only contains water, salt, and citric acid, or other legal ingredients, you might choose to try it.

Pineapple products, canned: Fresh pineapple is your best choice, but Dole pineapple that is canned in it's own juice is currently allowed, but be sure nothing else is added. In 2010 Dole added Vitamin A which was bound with illegal cornstarch (and wasn't mentioned on the label). After hearing from SCDers, they removed the Vitamin A (and cornstarch), but we have to be aware that products can change. Contact the company to be sure. You could substitute fresh orange juice for canned pineapple juice for a similar effect.

Pork, ground: Avoid any meat that contains natural flavors, broth, rosemary extract or any other illegals. Salt and water are okay. We have found pure ground pork at Walmart and Sprouts.

See p. 176

Note: This cookbook does not substitute for medical advice. We are sharing our personal experience with the Specific Carbohydrate Diet. Please read *Breaking the Vicious Cycle* by Elaine Gottschall for more complete information about the diet.

Pork Rinds: Unflavored pork rinds are a good substitute for chips.

Pumpkin Puree: Libby canned pumpkin is currently legal. You can be sure by making homemade pumpkin puree and freezing it or use homemade butternut squash puree.

Roasted Red bell pepper: You can easily roast your own (see instructions on p. 45) or if not new to the diet you might choose to buy bottled roasted red peppers that are free of illegal additives and only contain water, salt, and citric acid.

Sesame Seeds: May be added after a few months of initial success on the diet.

Tomatoes, diced: Canned tomatoes and tomato products such as tomato paste and tomato sauce often contain illegals from the canning process or the recipes used. It takes about 2 large tomatoes, diced, to equal a can of diced tomatoes and you can add a little legal tomato juice* if the recipe calls for undrained diced tomatoes. (See next entry) One legal brand is Pomi.

Tomato juice: Should only have salt and possibly a preservative such as citric acid added. We use Campbell's original brand.

Turkey, ground: Avoid any meat that contains natural flavors, broth, rosemary extract or any other illegals. Salt and water are okay. We have found pure ground turkey and chicken at Sprouts.

Vanilla: Water, alcohol, vanilla bean extractives (no sugars added)

Vinegar: Red and white wine vinegar, also white and cider vinegars are legal but carefully check the label for added illegals (usually sugars).

Yogurt, Homemade SCD: On a lactose-free diet you would think you couldn't eat yogurt, but that's not the case here. The yogurt made according to the directions on page 12, incubated at 100 to 110° Fahrenheit for a full 24-hours, has had the lactose digested away and is legal to eat.

See p. 165

Yogurt, Homemade, Dripped: Dripping yogurt makes it into thick Greek yogurt. Pour yogurt into a coffee-filter-lined strainer and place it over a tall saucepan. Refrigerate. A quick way to drip smaller amounts of yogurt is to place it between thick stacks of paper towels, flipping once, for 5 to 10 minutes. Scrape off with a rubber spatula. Dripped yogurt makes about half the amount you started with.

Yogurt Starter: Dannon All Natural full fat plain yogurt (with yogurt cultures and no additives such as pectin, etc.) *or* Yogourmet yogurt starter *or* GI Pro Health yogurt starter. Avoid starters with bifidus.

Yogurt maker, Luvele: This is the one Erin uses. It can keep the yogurt incubating at a steady 100° Fahrenheit for a 24-hour period, which is necessary to digest away all the lactose in the milk.

Ina Garten's Homemade Chicken Stock

Makes 4-6 quarts

- 3 (5-6 pound) whole chickens
- 3 large yellow onions, unpeeled and quartered
- 6 carrots, unpeeled, scrubbed and halved crosswise
- 4 celery stalks with leaves, cut into thirds crosswise
- 20 sprigs flat-leaf parsley
- 15 sprigs fresh thyme
- 8 sprigs fresh dill
- 1 whole head garlic, unpeeled and cut in half crosswise
- 2 Tbs. kosher salt
- 2 tsp. whole black peppercorns (not ground)

Place the chickens, onions, carrots, celery, parsley, thyme, dill, garlic, salt, and peppercorns in a 16 to 20-quart stockpot. Fill within a few inches of the top with water and bring to a boil. Lower the heat and simmer partially covered for 4 hours, skimming off any foam. Set aside until cool enough to handle. Remove large pieces of chicken, then strain broth through a large strainer into another pot and discard the solids. Cool meat enough to handle and remove from bones. Freeze for future meals. Freeze stock in quart size containers.

I like to include this adaptation of Ina Garten's Chicken Stock in all our cookbooks because it's so good! It's helpful to have a really good recipe for chicken stock, but don't forget you can always save and freeze the water you cook a chicken in for a simple broth.

Next time you have a food prep day, why not put this pot of ingredients on the back burner? Four hours later you'll have quarts of chicken stock to freeze, lots of cooked chicken meat to store in the freezer and the house will smell wonderful!

SCD Yogurt

Makes ½ Gallon

You will probably use this yogurt every day! It's a wonderful staple for the Specific Carbohydrate Diet, and is not difficult to make. Incubating the yogurt at 100 to 110° F. for 24 hours digests away all the lactose.

½ gallon of milk
½ c. yogurt starter*

Heat milk in a pan, stirring occasionally. When the temperature reaches 180°, turn heat off and allow milk to cool to 100-110° F. (Process may be hurried by placing pan in a sink of cold water and stirring until temp is reached.)

Meanwhile, if using a Yogourmet maker, add lukewarm water to the line indicated on your yogurt maker and plug it in to allow water to begin heating to the correct temperature.

Add starter* to yogurt container and set aside. When milk has cooled to 100-110° F., pour several cups of milk into yogurt container and mix yogurt starter and milk together well. Add the rest of the milk, and stir thoroughly. Put the lid on the yogurt container, and place in the yogurt maker.

(If using the Luvele yogurt maker, put the filled jar into the maker, fill to the top line with water, and turn it on.) Allow to incubate for **24 hours (max 30 hours)**. Remove yogurt container, chill in the refrigerator. Enjoy!

*Yogourmet yogurt starter packets may be used. See NoMoreCrohns.com Corner Grocery to buy starter or check your local health food store for these packets.

Tip: Erin has invested in two yogurt makers and three containers, which helps cut down on food prep time each month. She can make two more batches while she finishes the third container, and thus only needs to make yogurt twice a month! The yogurt maker and the jars, if used, are available on NoMoreCrohns.com.

I include this helpful recipe for yogurt in all our cookbooks because it's a staple food item for the SCD!

Navy Beans

Dried navy beans are delicious when cooked properly and are legal to try if you have been on the Specific Carbohydrate Diet for a few months. The simple tips below will help you cook up a perfect pot of beans that can be enjoyed now or frozen for later.

1. **Start with good quality beans.** Many bags on the supermarket shelves contain beans that are many years old, held in silos until they come to market. Health food stores and bulk sections may have a higher turn-over and fresher beans (even 1 to 2 years old is fine).

2. **Rinse and pick over the beans.** You're looking for dirt and pebbles from the field and dust from the silo or bulk bin. Give dried beans a quick rinse with cool water, then a quick once-over for any rare bits of rock hidden in the beans.

3. **Soak the beans overnight or for 10 to 12 hours.** This (and the fact that they aren't commercially canned) is what makes them SCD legal. Discard the soaking liquid and rinse the beans.

4. **Cover with fresh water and bring to a boil.** At this point you can add extra flavor to the beans by adding onion, carrot, celery or garlic to the pot if you will be using them in savory dishes.

5. **Reduce heat and simmer until beans are as tender as you like them.** This can take anywhere from 30 minutes for smaller, fresher beans to 2 hours for larger, older and drier beans.

6. **Add salt ¾ of the way through.** Salt can toughen bean skins, but a lack of salt creates tasteless beans. Adding salt when they are about ¾ of the way done avoids the toughening but adds the flavor. How to know when they're 3/4 done? When the beans start smelling like cooked beans and the beans are bite-able but not yet tender.

7. **Save and freeze the cooking liquid** to use as broth if you'd like to.

(Resource: localfoods.about.com)

I like to include this helpful information about navy beans in all our cookbooks because they're a staple food item for the SCD! Did you know you can always save and freeze the water you cook the beans in to use as a simple broth?

Background credit: FreePik

Appetizers & Drinks

Party Poppers, 16

Amaretto Cheese Apricots, 17

Bacon Wrapped Dates, 18

Carrot Curls, 19

Stuffed Mushrooms, 20

Chicken Satay Skewers, 21

Cheese Balls, 22

Melted Brie with Winter Fruits, 23

Fruit & Cheese Rolls, 24

Cheese Lace Crackers & Croutons, 25

Front Porch Pineapple Cheese Board, 26

Cucumber Limeade, 28

Ginger Pineapple Sparkling Punch, 29

Vitamix Basic Green Smoothie, 30

Strawberry Colada Smoothie, 31

Pumpkin Smoothie, 32

Frozen Fruit Smoothie, 33

Party Poppers
Makes 2 dozen

Use an interesting method to adjust the heat in these stuffed jalapeno peppers - adjust the amount of time you bake them to determine hot, medium, or mild. These hearty appetizers, adapted from Light & Tasty, will be a hit any time!

1¼ c. homemade yogurt*
12 jalapeno peppers
½ pound lean ground turkey*
¼ c. finely chopped onion
1-1/3 c. freshly grated Parmesan*, divided
1 Tbs. minced fresh cilantro
1 tsp. paprika
½ tsp. *each;* crushed garlic, cumin, and honey
1/8 tsp. *each;* salt and pepper

*See page 7 for an explanation of what makes this ingredient legal for the Specific Carbohydrate Diet.

Spread yogurt over a stack of thick paper towels, then top with another stack. Allow to rest for 5 to 10 minutes, turning once. Scrape off yogurt into a measuring cup and measure ½ c. Set aside. Save any remaining for another use.

Cut jalapenos in half lengthwise, leaving stems intact (wear gloves); discard seeds and membranes. Set aside. In a small nonstick skillet over medium heat, cook turkey and onion until meat is no longer pink; drain.

In a small bowl, combine the thickened yogurt, 1/3 c. parmesan cheese, cilantro, paprika, garlic, cumin, honey, salt, and pepper. Stir in turkey mixture. Spoon generously into pepper halves.

Place on an oiled baking sheet; sprinkle with remaining cheese. Bake, uncovered, at 350° for 20 minutes for spicy, 30 minutes for medium, and 40 minutes for mild.

Amaretto Cheese-Filled Apricots

Makes about 2 dozen

You get a lot of rich, sweet flavor in every little bite, in these stuffed apricots adapted from Healthy Cooking. They are perfect for a tea or special occasion.

- 1 (6 oz.) package dried pitted Mediterranean apricots or dried unsweetened apricot halves
- 1 c. homemade yogurt*
- ½ c. finely chopped unsalted almonds, toasted, divided
- ¼ c. dried unsweetened cherries, finely chopped
- ½ tsp. almond extract*
- 3 tsp. honey
- 1/8 tsp. orange zest

Spread yogurt over a stack of thick paper towels, then top with another stack. Allow to sit for 5 to 10 minutes, turning once, creating a simple yogurt cream cheese. Scrape the yogurt cream cheese with a rubber spatula into a small bowl.

Meanwhile, if using the whole, pitted apricots, gently loosen one of the long sides of each apricot, splitting to resemble clamshells. Whole dried apricots appear to be halves, but check along the edge for a place the seed was taken out or cut with a knife to separate.

Combine the yogurt cream cheese, ¼ c. almonds, cherries, almond extract, honey, and orange zest until blended. Chill for at least 30 minutes. Spoon 1¼ tsp. filling into each apricot. If using apricot halves, place filling between 2 halves and press together. Place remaining almonds in a small shallow dish; roll exposed cheese portions of apricots in nuts.

Bacon Wrapped Dates

This would be an excellent appetizer anytime for a party. We served these at Erin & Jim's wedding as part of the appetizer plates.

Stuff one **unsalted almond** into a **pitted date.** Wrap with half a slice of **pre-cooked bacon;** Hold it together with a toothpick. Bake in a 350 degree oven for about 15 minutes to warm date and crisp up bacon. (We use pre-cooked bacon from Costco.)

Carrot Curls

When you're craving chips, carrot curls are a satisfying, crunchy substitute! Recipe is from Breaking the Vicious Cycle.

Using a potato peeler, make thick curls out of about **3 large carrots** (or more carrots for desired amount).

Deep fry in **oil** until they turn golden brown. Using salad tongs or a slotted spoon, quickly remove them to a plate covered with several paper towels and salt & pepper them to taste.

After the cooking oil has cooled, strain the carrot bits out of it and refrigerate in a covered container for your next batch. The oil can be reused up to 3 times.

Food With Friends

Stuffed Mushrooms

Bacon Stuffed Mushrooms

30-35 large fresh mushrooms
¼ pound lean bacon, diced
1/3 c. diced red bell pepper
¼ c. diced red onion
1 tsp. minced garlic
½ tsp. *each;* salt and pepper
¼ c. crumbled Blue cheese*
¾ c. shredded Cheddar cheese*

Note: Each recipe is designed to use the larger mushrooms and if you use regular mushroom as we did for the photographs, you will have extra filling. One 8 oz. package of regular sized mushrooms contains about 15 to 17 mushrooms. We piled the leftover filling into small baking dishes and baked them alongside the mushrooms and were rewarded with two wonderful dips!

Rinse and dry mushrooms. Remove stems and finely chop; set caps aside. In a large skillet, cook bacon until cooked but not crisp. Remove all but one tablespoon of the grease. Add the chopped mushroom stems, red bell pepper, onion, garlic, salt, and pepper and continue cooking until vegetables are crisp-tender. Remove from heat and cool slightly. Stir in cheeses. Fill each mushroom cap with about 1 tablespoon of filling. Place on foil-lined baking sheets. Bake at 400° for 16-20 minutes or until mushrooms are tender.

Spinach Artichoke-Stuffed Mushrooms

1½ c. homemade yogurt*
½ c. homemade mayonnaise*, p. 176
1 bag (14 oz.) frozen artichoke hearts, boiled for 12 minutes, cooled & chopped
1 package (10 oz.) frozen chopped spinach, thawed & squeezed
1/3 c. freshly shredded Monterey Jack cheese*
4 Tbs. freshly shredded Parmesan cheese*
½ tsp. *each;* crushed garlic and salt
30-35 large fresh mushrooms

*See page 7 for an explanation of what makes this ingredient legal for the Specific Carbohydrate Diet.

Spread yogurt on several thicknesses of paper towels, then cover with several more. Allow to sit for 5 to 10 minutes, turning once. Scrape into a small mixing bowl and stir in mayonnaise, artichokes, spinach, Jack cheese, Parmesan cheese, garlic, and salt.

Rinse and dry mushrooms. Remove stems from mushrooms (discard stems or save for another use). Fill each mushroom cap with about 1 Tbs. of filling. Place on foil-lined baking sheets. Bake at 400° for 16-20 minutes or until mushrooms are tender.

Thai Chicken Satay

Makes 12-15 skewers

These delicious skewers of chicken make a great addition to any party or tapas meal. For tea size finger food we threaded on the meat, then cut the skewers in half with heavy kitchen shears. Recipe is adapted from cooks.com.

- **1 c. homemade yogurt***
- **½ c. unsweetened coconut milk***
- **1 Tbs. Homemade curry powder* (right)**
- **1 tsp. lemon juice**
- **1 tsp. grated fresh ginger**
- **½ tsp. salt**
- **½ tsp. black pepper**
- **1 clove garlic, crushed**
- **1 pound boneless, skinless chicken breasts (about 2)**
- **chopped fresh cilantro**
- **additional yogurt to serve**

Freeze the chicken for 30 to 60 minutes to make it easier to cut thin. Cut the chicken breasts to get long, thin strips that are about 1/8" thick and ½" wide. Thread strips onto soaked bamboo skewers, weaving the skewers in and out of the chicken, like a ribbon. Try to cover as much of the skewer as possible so the skewers don't burn under the broiler. Cut meat-threaded skewers in half with kitchen shears if you want small servings.

In a small bowl or pan, combine the yogurt, coconut milk, curry powder, lemon juice, ginger, salt, pepper, and garlic. Remove ½ cup of marinade to use as a dip. Submerge skewers in marinade, gently moving them around to make sure each one is covered with marinade. Cover and refrigerate for 3 to 4 hours, or if time is short, cover and place on the kitchen counter for up to 30 minutes.

Line up the satay skewers on a rimmed metal baking sheet. Broil about 6 inches from the heat for 2 to 4 minutes. (Be careful not to overcook.) Or, if desired, cook on a grill pan, turning once. Serve immediately.

Background credit: FreePik

Homemade Curry Powder

- **4 tsp. cumin**
- **4 tsp. coriander**
- **4 tsp. turmeric**
- **1 tsp. cinnamon**
- **1/2 tsp. nutmeg**
- **1/2 tsp. cayenne**
- **1/2 tsp. black pepper**
- **1/2 tsp. cloves**
- **1/2 tsp. cardamom**

Mix the spices together in a small labeled glass jar. Use as directed in this and other recipes.

Cheese Balls

Makes 2 balls

We love these cheese balls on New Year's Day, when we create a big spread of foods people can munch on all day while we watch the Rose Parade and the game. A crock pot full of legal pea soup, or chicken vegetable soup (see p. 11 for a great broth), fruit salad, veggies to dip, cheese cubes, crackers, p. 50, and Martinelli's Sparkling Cider or warm spiced cider* round out the menu. Yum! Make the cheese balls ahead so they have time to firm up.

Note: To create the pine cone shape, form cheese mixture into one cone shape, roll in chopped nuts, then press in toasted whole almonds to resemble a pine cone.

1 c. homemade yogurt*
½ c. butter, softened*
1 c. freshly grated Cheddar cheese*
1 c. freshly grated Monterey Jack cheese*
½ c. crumbled blue cheese*
1 green onion, finely chopped
pecans or walnuts, finely chopped

Pour yogurt onto a stack of paper towels and cover with another stack. Allow to sit for 5 to 10 minutes, turning once. Scrape yogurt cheese into a mixing bowl. Place chopped nuts on a plate and set aside.

To the yogurt cheese, add softened butter, Cheddar, and Jack cheeses. Combine with an electric mixer until well mixed. Use a rubber spatula to fold in blue cheese and green onion.

Shape cheese into two balls, (making two smaller balls keeps them looking tidier, after everyone starts digging in, than one big ball) using the spatula to help if needed; roll balls in finely chopped nuts, pressing nuts into cheese and forming a nice ball shape. Refrigerate until firm, then wrap in plastic wrap until time to serve.

To serve, place one ball in the middle of a plate and surround with assorted vegetables such as bell pepper strips, mushrooms, cucumber slices, baby carrots, and celery sticks. Have a small cheese knife nearby.

Appetizers & Drinks

Baked Brie with Winter Fruits

Makes 6-8 servings

Spread warm brie with softened fruit filling on small circles of Easy Sandwich Bread, p. 40, cucumber circles, thin apple slices, or diagonally sliced carrots. Provide crackers for everyone, p. 50. This recipe is a winner and is adapted from Sunset's "International Cooking."

- ¾ c. chopped pitted unsweetened dates
- 1 *each;* small apple and small firm-ripe pear, peeled, cored, and diced
- ½ c. currants or chopped dark raisins
- ½ c. chopped pecans
- 1/3 c. apple cider*
- 1 wedge ripe Brie, well chilled
- breads or veggies for dipping, p. 35

In a bowl, mix dates, apple, pear, currants or raisins, pecans, and cider. Set aside to soften fruit, about 2 hours.

Cut brie in half to make two layers. Place 1 layer, cut side up, in an attractive 10-inch shallow-rimmed baking dish (such as a quiche pan). Spread cut side with half of the fruit. Place remaining cheese layer, cut side down, on fruit. Spoon remaining fruit onto center of cheese. If made ahead, cover and chill filled cheese up to two days.

Bake brie, uncovered, in a 350° oven until it melts at the edges and center is warm, 25-30 minutes. Offer hot brie from baking dish; scoop up cheese with a knife to spread.

*See page 7 for an explanation of what makes this ingredient legal for the Specific Carbohydrate Diet.

Background credit: FreePik

Fruit & Cheese Rolls

Makes 2 logs

Like a cheese ball, but with sweet notes from dried fruit and orange zest.

> 1 c. homemade yogurt*
> ½ c. butter, softened*
> 1 c. freshly grated sharp Cheddar cheese*
> 1 c. freshly grated Monterey Jack cheese*
> ¾ c. finely chopped dried mixed fruit
> 1 tsp. orange zest
> ½ c. toasted unsweetened coconut

Note: Serve with apple slices, assorted vegetables, breads, p. 35, and Cheese Lace Crackers.

To toast coconut, stir it constantly in a dry skillet over medium heat just until it begins to brown. Pour onto a plate.

Place yogurt between two thick stacks of paper towels. Allow to rest 5 to 10 minutes, turning over once. Remove thickened yogurt with a rubber spatula. Measure ½ cup for this recipe.

In a large bowl, beat butter until smooth. Add yogurt, Cheddar, Jack, dried fruit, and orange zest; blend well. Refrigerate mixture 30 to 60 minutes or until easy to handle. Using waxed paper, roll mixture into two 6-inch logs. Refrigerate until firm, about 1 hour. Roll in toasted coconut.

Cheese Lace Crackers & Croutons

Cheddar Cheese* (Jack and Parmesan also taste great)
Oil

To microwave: Apply a thick layer of oil to a pyrex pie pan, or other glazed non-stick glass plate. Cover plate with medium slices of cheese. Cook in microwave for approximately three minutes (depending on your microwave), until cheese is thoroughly cooked and has a crackly top all over. Immediately and carefully remove from microwave and tip to one side to dab up the oil with several napkins. Break into chip-sized pieces and enjoy with salsa, guacamole, or any other SCD dip!

To bake: For croutons or crackers, cut desired cheese into cubes, then place, 2 inches apart, on a parchment lined sheet pan. Bake at 350° for 7-12 minutes, or until edges are starting to brown.

Notes: If you bake the cheese, be sure to line pan with parchment only - foil won't work.

If you take them out of the oven too soon, they'll just be stretchy melted cheese, not cheese "crisps."

You can also grate your cheese and combine cheeses or add pinches of spices - just don't add salt! Cheese is already salty.

*See page 7 for an explanation of what makes this ingredient legal for the Specific Carbohydrate Diet.

Food With Friends

Front Porch Pineapple Cheese Board

Serves 6-10

Our world would be a better place if we could think of more easy ways to serve food to others! We could more readily open our hearts, homes, and front porches to friends and neighbors and just sit down with a glass of iced tea and enjoy them. How nice!

We often have items on hand or in the freezer that we can put together to make a tasty cheese board, and this includes fresh fruit, dried fruit, cheeses, breads, and nuts. Choose some from each category suggested below when you assemble your board.

Start with a **fresh pineapple**, cut into wedges, placing the top in the center.

Cheeses: At three corners of the board, place cheeses such as Babybel cheddar cheeses, wedges of brie, a cheese ball, p. 22, sliced or cubed cheddar or other legal cheeses you have on hand. Stick toothpicks in the cheese cubes to make eating easier.

Breads: Near the cheeses, place two or three breads (these can be made ahead and frozen), including some that are non-SCD in a separate vessel:

- Best Banana Nut Bread slices, p. 38
- Garlic Cheese Pizza Crust, cut into wedges, p. 42
- Socca Flatbread, cut into wedges, p. 44
- Rosemary Thyme Crackers, p. 50
- Cheese Lace Crackers, p. 25
- Grain-Free Focaccia Bread, p. 81
- Regular crackers and rolls in a basket on the side for non-SCDers and people with nut allergies.

Fresh stuff: In between, tumble piles of fresh cherries, strawberries, watermelon wedges, orange slices, or bunches of grapes.

Nuts: Fill in with little handfuls or dishes of nuts, such as pistachios in shells, raw cashews, toasted pecans, walnuts, or almonds.

Dried Fruit: Here and there, tuck in small bunches of dried fruit such as apricots, peaches, figs, or dates.

Fill in with fresh rosemary sprigs, parsley, or other fresh herbs.

Note: Lay a cheese knife by the brie or cheese ball and put a stack of little plates and napkins nearby.

See page 7 for an explanation of what makes this ingredient legal for the Specific Carbohydrate Diet.

Cucumber Limeade

Makes about 9 cups.

Gather on the porch or the patio with some fresh snacks and enjoy this refreshing, earthy tasting beverage from BHG at a low-stress get-together!

In a blender pulse one sliced **cucumber** and ¼ c. **water** to break it up; blend on high until liquefied. (Cucumber has a high water content so very little extra water is needed.) Strain through a fine-mesh sieve into a pitcher, pressing to extract juice. Discard solids. Add 1 cup fresh **lime juice**, and ½ cup **honey**. Stir thoroughly and chill. To serve, add 7 cups **cold water.** Garnish with lime and cucumber slices.

Ginger Pineapple Sparkling Punch

Makes 1½ gallons

Adapted from epicurious, this punch will disappear in a hurry!

For ginger syrup:
- 1½ c. water
- 1 c. honey
- 1 c. thinly sliced unpeeled fresh ginger - ¼ lb.

For punch:
- 3 c. unsweetened pineapple juice, chilled*
- ¼ c. fresh lemon juice
- ¼ c. fresh lime juice
- 3 to 4 c. club soda, chilled
- 4 c. ice cubes

Photo credit: Pexels

To make ginger syrup, bring water, honey, and ginger to a boil. Reduce heat and simmer, uncovered, stirring occasionally, 10 minutes. Remove from heat and cool completely. Pour syrup through a sieve into a measuring cup or saucepan, discarding ginger. Chill until cold, about two hours or up to two weeks.

To make punch, stir together the ginger syrup and fruit juices in a punch bowl or pitcher. Gently stir in club soda and ice before serving.

See page 7 for an explanation of what makes this ingredient legal for the Specific Carbohydrate Diet.

Vitamix Basic Green Smoothie

Serves 4

This is now Erin's favorite smoothie for herself and her kids. It makes a quick snack! She has adapted it from the Vitamix cookbook, but this is the smoothie that made her want to get a Vitamix for herself! The citrus adds such a bright taste and "hides" the taste of the spinach.

- **zest of one small lime**
- **1 speckled banana, peeled**
- **1½ c. green grapes**
- **4 tangerines** *or* **1 orange, peeled, halved, and seeded**
- **1½ c. spinach, or more**
- **1½ c. frozen pineapple**
- **2 Tbs. honey**
- **½ c. water**
- **1 c. crushed ice**

Place all ingredients into the Vitamix container in the order listed and secure the lid. Select variable 1. Turn machine on and slowly increase speed to variable 10, then to High. Blend 30 seconds, or until desired consistency.

We used purple grapes, but if you use green grapes, the color will be a beautiful, bright green.

Strawberry Colada Smoothie

Serves 3-4

A refreshing and beautiful smoothie adapted from cookingclassy! A sweet coconut milk and fruit mixture is swirled together with strawberry puree. Not hard to make and so delicious!

> 8 oz. fresh strawberries, chilled and hulled
> 1 speckled banana, peeled and frozen
> 1½ c. frozen pineapple chunks*
> scant 1 c. homemade yogurt*
> 1½ c. unsweetened coconut milk*
> ¼ c. honey
> ¾ c. crushed ice

Pulse strawberries in a food processor until pureed. Pour into a container and set aside. Rinse the food processor and add banana, and remaining ingredients. Pulse until well blended.

Spoon some pineapple mixture into three to four glasses, filling about 1/3 full, then add a spoonful or two of the strawberry puree, swirling lightly with a dinner knife and pushing some to the edges. Repeat twice more. Alternatively, all ingredients can be blended together in a blender for a pretty pink smoothie. Serve immediately.

*See page 7 for an explanation of what makes this ingredient legal for the Specific Carbohydrate Diet.

Food With Friends

Autumn Pumpkin Smoothie

Serves 3-4

Note: When you have too many ripe bananas, peel, break them in half and freeze in zip-top bags for when you want to pull one out to make a quick, thick, smoothie.

- 2 c. pumpkin puree*
- ½ c. homemade yogurt*
- ½ c. almond milk* *or* combine ¼ c. homemade yogurt and water to equal ½ c.
- 1 speckled* banana, peeled & frozen
- 1 tsp. cinnamon
- ¾ tsp. ginger
- ¼ tsp. nutmeg
- ¼ c. honey (or more to taste)
- ½ c. crushed ice

Blend all until thick, completely smooth and frothy.

Image credit: Pexels

Frozen Fruit Smoothie

Serves 3-4

Use what you have on hand to make this refreshing and nutrient packed smoothie for a hot summer day, adapted from dinneratthezoo.

- 1½ c. fruit juice such as apple cider*, white grape juice*, orange juice
- 2 c. assorted frozen fruit such as cherries, raspberries, blueberries, pineapple, and/or mango
- ¾ c. homemade yogurt*
- 1 Tbs. honey
- ½ tsp. vanilla*
- additional fruit and/or mint sprigs for garnish (opt.)

Place the juice, fruit, yogurt, honey, and vanilla in a blender. Blend until completely smooth. Pour into three or four short glasses. Garnish with additional fruit and mint sprigs if desired.

*See page 7 for an explanation of what makes this ingredient legal for the Specific Carbohydrate Diet.

Food With Friends

Background credit: FreePik

Breads & Muffins

Apple Ginger Spice Scones, 36

Best Banana Bread, 38

Protein Bread, 39

Erin's Easy Sandwich Bread, 40

English Muffins, 41

Grain-Free Focaccia Bread, 81

Garlic Cheese Pizza Crust, 42

Pizza Bread Rounds, 43

Socca Flatbread & Toppings, 44

Socca Tortillas, 49

Rosemary Thyme Crackers, 50

Nacho Cheese Triangles, 51

Very Lemon Muffins, 52

Lemon Poppy Seed Muffins, 53

Orange Spice Muffins & Donuts, 54

Blueberry Streusel Muffins, 55

Apple Ginger Spice Scones

Makes 12 scones

Fresh from the oven these scones are heavenly with a cup of tea. Serve at your holiday brunch or tea!

2½ c. almond flour
½ c. coconut flour, sifted
1 tsp. *each;* baking soda and cinnamon
½ tsp. nutmeg
½ c. sliced toasted almonds
1 c. 24 hours dripped homemade yogurt* (see note, left)
3 Tbs. melted butter*
4 Tbs. honey
3 eggs
1 tsp *each;* almond extract* and vanilla extract*
1 Tbs. grated fresh ginger
1 c. sweet apple, peeled and finely chopped

Preheat oven to 350° and place parchment on a baking sheet. Combine flours, soda, cinnamon, nutmeg, and toasted almonds; set aside.

Mix yogurt cheese, butter, honey, eggs, extracts, and ginger together in a food processor.

Transfer yogurt mixture to a large bowl and stir in the flour mixture. Gently mix in the apples. Transfer to the baking sheet and shape into two lightly flattened circles; cut each circle into 6 triangles, separating slightly. Smooth each one with a wet finger, and bake for 15 minutes.

Note: To make 1 cup of dripped yogurt cheese, place about 2 cups homemade yogurt in a large coffee-filter-lined strainer over a deep saucepan. Refrigerate for 24 hours. Will be almost as dense as cream cheese.

See page 7 for an explanation of what makes this ingredient legal for the Specific Carbohydrate Diet.

Breads & Muffins

Scone is topped with orange butter, made by combining softened butter*, honey and orange zest to taste.

Background credit: FreePik

Best Banana Nut Bread

Makes 2 medium loaves

Nice and firm, you'll really enjoy these sweet loaves! Our tasters didn't care if this recipe used coconut flour, lots of eggs, or if it was SCD legal, they just wanted more of it. You and your people will too! Freeze a loaf to bring out when you're throwing together a spur-of-the-moment snack with friends!

1 speckled banana* or 4 speckled baby bananas
8 eggs
½ c. homemade yogurt*
½ c. honey
½ tsp. vanilla*
1 tsp. almond extract*
½ tsp. salt
¾ c. sifted coconut flour
1 tsp. baking soda
¾ c. pecans or walnuts, chopped

*See page 7 for an explanation of what makes this ingredient legal for the Specific Carbohydrate Diet.

Grease two 7x3-inch loaf pans with oil or real butter. Line bottom of pans with parchment or waxed paper. Preheat oven to 325°.

In a large bowl, with an electric mixer, blend together mashed banana, eggs, yogurt, honey, vanilla, almond extract, and salt. Combine coconut flour with baking soda and beat thoroughly into egg mixture until there are no lumps. Fold in nuts. Mixture will be thinner than you expect.

Pour into prepared pans and bake for 45-55 minutes or until a toothpick inserted in the center of the loaf comes out clean. Remove from oven and cool on a rack or unused stove burner where air can circulate around the loaves.

Photo credit: Ian @ Pexels

Protein Bread

Makes 16 Slices

Adapted for the SCD from the FatForWeightLoss keto website, this bread is excellent for sandwiches or toast! It resembles normal wheat bread in texture and each slice contains 6 g of protein, 3g of carbs and about 165 calories. We made our loaf in an 8x4-inch pan.

- **7 large eggs, at room temperature to reduce eggy taste (may be warmed for 3 minutes in a bowl of hot tap water)**
- **½ c. butter*, cut up and just melted over low heat or in microwave**
- **2 Tbs. coconut oil, added to warmed butter**
- **2 c. almond flour**
- **1 Tbs. coconut flour**
- **½ tsp. baking soda**
- **¾ tsp. salt**

Preheat oven to 355° (335° if using a glass loaf pan, which retains heat longer). Grease loaf pan and line completely with two strips of parchment going both directions so pan is completely covered. Combine almond flour, coconut flour, baking soda, and salt with a fork; set aside.

Crack eggs into a bowl and beat for 1 to 2 minutes on high. Slowly stream the warm, not hot, coconut oil and melted butter mixture into the eggs, beating on low speed. (You won't want the butter to be hot because this will cook the eggs when you combine them.)

With beater running, add flour mixture little by little to the egg mixture, beating well after each addition.

Spoon some dough into prepared loaf pan, pushing paper into position. Pour in remaining dough. Bake for 35 to 45 minutes. Once cracks appear on the top and it turns golden brown, test with a toothpick in the center of the bread. If it comes out clean, the bread is done. If not, add more time, checking until done.

Let the bread cool on a cooling rack or unused stove-top burner so all sides cool equally. Cooling it on a rack will significantly reduce the eggy taste.

Slice into 16 thin slices, and store in an airtight container in the fridge for up to 7 days, or up to 1 month in the freezer.

Background credit: FreePik

Erin's Easy Sandwich Bread

Serves 4

Erin's husband Jim created this yummy recipe for fluffy, easy sandwich bread. She tried it and immediately wanted to make a sandwich using peanut butter* and homemade jam! Next she had PB & honey… just like the good ole' days! And don't forget grilled cheese sandwiches! Yum.

- ½ c. homemade yogurt*
- 4 eggs
- 2 c. almond flour
- ½ tsp. salt
- ½ tsp. baking soda
- ¼ c. Cheddar cheese*, diced

Note: These are very light and fluffy and taste best toasted. Great with tuna* salad, egg salad, or as a grilled cheese sandwich.

*See page 7 for an explanation of what makes this ingredient legal for the Specific Carbohydrate Diet.

Mix all ingredients in a blender until smooth. Pour in round circles on an electric griddle (preferably), heated to 250°F. You can also use a skillet. Cook until golden brown on both sides. Place on a baking sheet to cool, and store breads in gallon-sized zip top bags.

For extended storage, freeze and defrost one at a time in the microwave. Toast.

English Muffins

Makes 1 muffin

¼ c. almond flour
1 Tbs. coconut flour
¼ tsp. baking soda
1/8 tsp. salt

1 egg white
½ tsp. coconut oil
2 Tbs. hot water

For a Cinnamon-Raisin version, add:
¼ tsp. cinnamon
½ Tbs. honey
1½ Tbs. raisins

Mix dry ingredients together in a small ramekin or other microwave-safe bowl. Add wet ingredients and mix well. Microwave for two minutes. Remove, slice in half, and toast or broil until golden brown.

Serve with butter or homemade jam, legal peanut butter - or any other SCD spread! This would work great for an egg, bacon & cheese breakfast sandwich or BLT.

Note from Erin: "When we travel, I have brought along all the ingredients for individual muffins in small baggies, except for the egg whites and hot water, which I added at the hotel (we carry eggs in our cooler). We also took along a bowl to cook it in, and since we get rooms with microwaves, I can enjoy these muffins for breakfast at our hotels!"

For at-home use, you could make a week's worth of baggies and quickly cook yourself a muffin each morning or just make a bunch on your prep day and freeze for later.

Garlic Cheese Pizza Crust

Makes 2 large personal sized pizza crusts

Make these lovely crusts for a pizza party, p. 64! It might be a good idea to double the recipe - other people might want to try them. You can get Naan bread or other flatbreads for the non-SCDers.

See baking notes and tips on page 70.

1½ c. freshly grated Monterey Jack cheese*, lightly compressed
3 Tbs. butter*
½ tsp. crushed garlic
1½ c. almond flour
1 tsp. baking soda
1 egg, beaten with a fork

Preheat oven to 425°. Combine almond flour and baking soda; stir to remove lumps; set aside. Place a piece of parchment paper on a baking sheet; sprinkle on about 2 teaspoons of **coconut flour**.

Combine Jack cheese, butter, and garlic in a large saucepan. Cook on high, stirring constantly, 1 minute. Cook up to 30 more seconds, just until melted (this may also be done in a microwave). Stir 10 to 15 times to cool slightly. Vigorously stir in egg to keep it from cooking when it touches warm cheese; add almond flour mixture, stirring until dough forms a ball.

Turn dough out onto prepared parchment and knead a few times; cut into two pieces. Pat each piece into a flat shape. Bake for 6 minutes, turn pan, then bake 3 more minutes until brown. Put on toppings of your choice and bake for 8-12 minutes or until cheese is melted.

Pizza Bread Rounds

Makes 4 5-inch rounds or 1 large pizza crust

Crispy and firm, this bread uses cheese, coconut flour, and almond flour to make great bread rounds for everything from sandwiches to mini pizza crusts. Butter a piece and eat it with your favorite soup! The recipe is adapted from Tropical Traditions.

- **2 c. Cheddar and/or Monterey Jack cheese***
- **2 large eggs, lightly beaten**
- **2 Tbs. almond flour**
- **2 Tbs. coconut flour**
- **½ tsp.** *each;* **baking soda and salt**
- **1 tsp. fresh lemon juice**

Preheat oven to 350°. Cut 2 pieces of parchment paper for baking sheet if making the large pizza crust. Otherwise, cut one piece of parchment paper.

Combine cheese, eggs, almond flour, coconut flour, baking soda, and lemon juice until a wet dough is formed. Form into 4 balls; place on parchment lined sheet pan and press flat, to about ½-inch thickness.

Bake for 30 minutes in preheated oven. Halfway through the baking process, flip breads over with a spatula. Return to oven to finish baking.

If making the large pizza crust, flip crust by sliding it and the parchment off the baking sheet, placing the second parchment on the baking sheet and turning the crust over onto the new parchment. Remove old parchment and return to oven to finish baking.

*See page 7 for an explanation of what makes this ingredient legal for the Specific Carbohydrate Diet.

Food With Friends

Socca Flatbread & Toppings

Makes 5 socca

Socca is a popular street food in the south of France, is savory and perfect paired with flavorful toppings (following pages). Socca flatbreads are not hard to make and taste great with a little char on them. Serving socca and toppings, along with some cheese, fruit, and hard boiled eggs, makes a fun finger-food meal, with everyone reaching and trying the different toppings. This meal is a delicious conversation starter in itself!

Note: Normally made with starchy garbanzo bean flour, our flavorful socca flatbreads are made with almond and coconut flours and cheese. You'll love the fresh and tasty go-withs that follow, which are from BHG!

Kneading in the coconut flour gives socca a more stable texture.

See additional baking notes on page 70.

1½ c. almond flour
1 tsp. baking soda
½ tsp. *each;* salt and smoked paprika
1 Tbs. chopped rosemary leaves
1½ c. freshly grated Monterey Jack cheese*, lightly compressed
3 Tbs. olive oil
1 clove garlic, minced
1 egg, beaten well with a fork

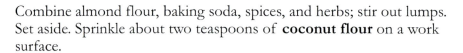

5 tsp. oil

*See page 7 for an explanation of what makes this ingredient legal for the Specific Carbohydrate Diet.

Combine almond flour, baking soda, spices, and herbs; stir out lumps. Set aside. Sprinkle about two teaspoons of **coconut flour** on a work surface.

Combine cheese, oil, and garlic in a large saucepan. Cook and stir over medium heat until cheese is just melted, about 1 to 1½ minutes. Stir 10 to 15 times to cool slightly, then vigorously stir in the egg to keep it from cooking when it touches the warm cheese. Add almond flour mixture, stirring until dough holds together. Turn dough onto work surface and knead a few times, then cut into 5 portions.

Meanwhile, preheat broiler and set rack so bottom of 10-inch cast iron skillet is 5 inches below the heat. Add 1 tsp. of the oil to the skillet and place in the broiler to preheat for 5 minutes.

Roll one ball of dough between two pieces of parchment until about the size of a salad plate, about ¼-inch thick.

Using hot pads, remove skillet and drop flattened dough into hot skillet. Return skillet to broiler and broil for 1 to 1½ minutes until golden brown and charred in some areas. Transfer to paper towels. Repeat with remaining dough, adding 1 tsp. oil to hot pan before cooking each socca. Serve at room temperature or reheat socca in 350° oven on baking sheet for 5 minutes. Cut rounds in half or into triangles.

Rosemary Photo credit: MarksDailyApple

Olive Relish

Makes about 2 cups

May be made up to one week ahead.

1 c. green olives*, chopped
½ c. black olives, such as Kalamata, pitted and chopped (check for pit fragments)
2 Tbs. red bell pepper, finely chopped
1 Tbs. olive oil
2 tsp. orange zest
1 tsp. fresh thyme leaves
1 clove garlic, minced
½ tsp. crushed red pepper
¾ tsp. salt

In small bowl combine all ingredients until well mixed. Serve at room temperature, or cover and chill up to 1 week. Serve with socca.

Smoky Carrot Spread

Makes about 2 cups

3 Tbs. olive oil
1 pound carrots, peeled and sliced
2 cloves garlic, peeled and chopped
1 roasted red bell pepper, peeled, stemmed, and seeded (right)
   or ¾ c. bottled roasted red bell pepper*
1/8 to ¼ tsp. hot pepper sauce*
2 tsp. smoked paprika
2 Tbs. red wine vinegar*

In a large skillet heat 2 Tbs. of the oil over medium-low heat. Add carrots and garlic; cook and stir 12 minutes or until carrots are caramelized and tender. (May be refrigerated for 24 hours.)

Transfer carrots, garlic, and any oil to blender. Add roasted pepper, hot sauce, paprika, vinegar, and the remaining 1 Tbs. oil. Cover; blend until smooth, scraping sides as necessary. Season to taste with **salt**. Transfer to a serving bowl; drizzle with additional olive oil. Serve with socca.

Note: Roast bell peppers by placing whole peppers on a foil lined sheet pan. Roast in a preheated 425° oven for about 20 minutes, or until covered with charred spots. Pull foil up around peppers and seal to create steam which loosens skins. When cool, remove skins, stems, and seeds and use as directed.

Chile Zucchini Topper

Makes 4 servings

None of our tasters realized there was a jalapeno in this topper, and it was a favorite with everyone.

- ¼ c. chopped fresh mint
- 3 Tbs. olive oil
- 2 Tbs. red wine vinegar*
- 1 fresh jalapeno chile pepper, seeded, stemmed, and finely minced (wear gloves)
- 1 clove garlic, minced
- ½ tsp. salt
- 2 medium zucchini, sliced into ¼-inch thick rounds

In a jar, shake together mint, 2 Tbs. of the olive oil, vinegar, jalapeno, garlic, and salt. Set dressing aside.

Place zucchini in a plastic zip-top bag and add remaining 1 Tbs. oil. Sprinkle lightly with salt. Squish around so that all the zucchini pieces are covered with oil.

Using tongs, arrange zucchini on an oiled grill pan over medium heat in a few batches. Grill 1 to 2 minutes per side or until charred and softened. Remove to serving bowl. Spoon dressing over zucchini. Serve with socca.

Sweet-Spicy Cherries

Makes 6 servings

We made this almost a week ahead. Our tasters didn't feel any heat from the one large jalapeno, but it added depth of flavor to this delicious condiment, and everyone loved it.

- ½ c. red wine vinegar*
- ¼ c. honey
- 1½ c. fresh or frozen dark sweet cherries, pitted and halved
- 1 to 2 jalapeno chile peppers, seeded, stemmed, and finely diced (wear gloves)
- ½ small red onion, halved, quartered, and thinly sliced

In a small saucepan combine vinegar, honey, and ¼ tsp. **kosher salt**. Bring just to a boil over medium heat, stirring to dissolve honey; reduce heat. Simmer, uncovered, 2 minutes. Remove from heat.

Meanwhile, in a medium bowl combine cherries, jalapenos, and onion. Pour hot vinegar mixture over cherry mixture; stir to combine. Cover; let stand at least 15 minutes or refrigerate up to one week to soften onion and combine flavors. Serve at room temperature, draining most of the vinegar mixture before serving. Serve with socca.

*See page 7 for an explanation of what makes this ingredient legal for the Specific Carbohydrate Diet.

Caramelized Onions

Makes about 2 cups

- 3 large onions, halved and sliced very thin
- 4 Tbs. butter*
- 1 Tbs. honey

Melt butter in a large non-stick skillet over medium low heat, then fill pan with onions. Stir until onions are coated with butter. Turn heat to low; continue cooking, stirring occasionally, for 10 minutes. Drizzle with the honey. Stir, and continue cooking until onions are turning golden brown, about 20 to 30 more minutes. Serve with socca.

Heidi's Socca Tortillas

Makes 8

My daughter Heidi built on our socca flatbread recipe and created these wonderful food wraps for her husband, who wants to cut carbs! Pliable and delicious, these "tortillas" hold up well when filled with taco fillings and can be wrapped and stored in the fridge for a few days.

- 1½ c. almond flour
- 1 Tbs. coconut flour + 2 tsp. more for kneading
- 1 tsp. baking soda
- ½ tsp. *each;* salt and smoked paprika
- 1½ c. freshly grated Monterey Jack cheese*, lightly compressed
- 3 Tbs. olive oil
- 1 clove garlic, minced
- 1 egg, beaten well with a fork
- Oil to grease the skillet

Combine almond flour, coconut flour, baking soda, and spices; stir out all lumps. Set aside. Sprinkle about 2 teaspoons of coconut flour on a work surface.

Combine cheese, oil, and garlic in a large saucepan. Cook and stir over medium heat until cheese is just melted, about 1 to 1½ minutes. (You may also do this in the microwave.) Stir 10 to 15 times to cool slightly, then vigorously stir in the egg to keep it from cooking when it touches the warm cheese. Add flour mixture, stirring until dough holds together. Turn dough onto floured work surface and knead a few times, then cut into 8 portions.

*See page 7 for an explanation of what makes this ingredient legal for the Specific Carbohydrate Diet.

Meanwhile, heat a 10-inch cast iron skillet over medium heat. Add oil to skillet and allow pan to become very hot.

Roll one ball of dough between two pieces of parchment paper until about the size of a salad plate, about 1/8-inch thick. (May cut into a circle if desired.)

Drop flattened dough into hot skillet. Cook for about 1 minute, then flip over and cook until golden brown and charred in some areas. Transfer to paper towels. Repeat with remaining dough. Hang over a wooden spoon to help create the folded shape. May wrap and refrigerate, then reheat quickly and reshape if needed.

Rosemary Thyme Crackers

Makes 25-30 crackers

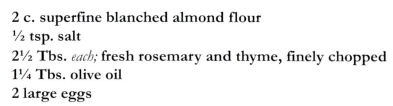

My daughter Gretchen makes these crackers from the recipe on the Walmart almond flour bag. They are easy and taste great!

    2 c. superfine blanched almond flour
    ½ tsp. salt
    2½ Tbs. *each;* fresh rosemary and thyme, finely chopped
    1¼ Tbs. olive oil
    2 large eggs

Preheat oven to 350°. In a large bowl, combine almond flour, salt, rosemary, and thyme. In a medium bowl, whisk together the olive oil and the egg. Combine wet ingredients into the almond flour and mix until fully integrated.

Roll the dough into a ball and press between two sheets of parchment paper to desired thickness. Remove top piece of parchment paper. Transfer the bottom piece and the dough onto a baking sheet. Cut dough into squares with a knife or a pizza cutter. (Dough could be re-covered with the top piece of parchment and refrigerated for a few hours at this point.)

Bake at 350° for 12-15 minutes or until slightly golden. Let the crackers cool on a baking sheet for 30 minutes and then serve.

Thyme Photo credit:
MarksDailyApple

Nacho Cheese Triangles

Makes 16 wedges

Make these munchy, cheesy goodies for the weekend football game! Adapted from Elana'spantry, they are perfect with guacamole.

- 2 c. stirred almond flour
- ½ tsp. salt
- 1 tsp. *each;* baking soda and paprika (smoky or sweet)
- 1 tsp. ground dried chiles*
- 2 ¾ c. white or yellow Cheddar cheese*
- 1 egg, whisked

In a large bowl, combine almond flour, salt, soda, paprika, ground pepper and most of the cheese, breaking up any lumps.

Stir egg into flour mixture with a fork. Knead dough with hands if necessary to ensure proper distribution of ingredients, adding a few drops of water if needed so dough forms a ball. Press dough into a circle about 8 inches across. Cut dough into 16 wedges.

Using a metal baking spatula, transfer triangles to a parchment-lined baking sheet leaving some space around each. Sprinkle with remaining cheese. Bake at 375° for 9 to 11 minutes, until cheese is melting and triangles are beginning to brown. Remove to a rack to cool.

Background credit: FreePik

*See page 7 for an explanation of what makes this ingredient legal for the Specific Carbohydrate Diet.

Food With Friends

Very Lemon Muffins

Makes about 20-22 mini muffins

Little lemon "hats" add a fun touch to these great muffins, based on a recipe from Elana'sPantry, and would be perfect to serve at a tea.

¼ c. coconut flour
¼ tsp. salt
¼ tsp. baking soda
3 eggs
¼ c. honey
¼ c. grapeseed oil
3 Tbs. lemon zest

Photo credit: Pexels

2 medium lemons, one for zest, above, and one to slice
½ c. water
¼ c. honey

*See page 7 for an explanation of what makes this ingredient legal for the Specific Carbohydrate Diet.

Combine coconut flour, salt, and baking soda and set aside.

In a large bowl, blend together eggs, ¼ c. honey, oil, and lemon zest. Blend dry ingredients into egg mixture.

Spoon 1 Tbs. batter into each well greased mini muffin cup. Bake at 350° for 8 to 10 minutes.

Meanwhile, cut lemon into paper thin slices, removing seeds. Place slices in a saucepan with ¼ c. honey and ½ c. water. Bring to a boil and simmer for 10 minutes, or until syrup is very thick. Using tongs, remove slices to a rack to cool and dry. Save syrup.

When muffins are done, remove from oven and cool for a few minutes, then drizzle ¼ tsp. syrup on top of each muffin. If you still have more syrup, go back and add more syrup to muffin tops. Serve muffins, some topped with candied lemon slices and some without.

Lemon Poppyseed Muffins

Makes 6 regular muffins

Try these amazing muffins! The recipe is adapted from Elana's Pantry and will make an SCDer's heart sing.

- ¼ c. coconut flour
- ¼ tsp salt
- ¼ tsp. baking soda
- 3 eggs
- ¼ c. honey
- ¼ c. ghee or grapeseed oil
- 1 Tbs. lemon zest
- 1 Tbs. poppy seeds

Combine coconut flour, salt and baking soda and set aside.

In a large bowl, blend together eggs, honey, oil, and lemon zest. Blend dry ingredients into the egg mixture. Fold in poppy seeds.

Divide between 6 greased or paper-lined muffin cups. Bake at 350° for 8 to 10 minutes. Cool and serve.

Food With Friends

Orange Spice Muffins & Donuts with Buttercream Icing

Makes 12 regular muffins or donuts or 48 mini muffins

Using part of a whole cooked and pureed orange gives delicious orange flavor to these muffins or donuts! The mixture makes a great stand-in for orange juice concentrate and any leftovers can be frozen for when you want deep orange flavor.

    1 whole medium orange, including peel (use as directed)
    6 eggs
    4 Tbs. homemade yogurt*
    1 tsp. vanilla*
    ½ c. honey
    ¼ c. raisins or chopped dates
    ½ c. coconut flour, lightly stirred
    3 tsp. cinnamon
    1 tsp. nutmeg
    ¼ tsp. cloves
    ½ tsp. *each;* **salt and baking soda**
    4 Tbs. orange zest, plus more for garnish, if desired
    1 c. pecans, finely chopped, plus more for garnish, if desired

Boil whole orange in water to cover for 90 minutes. Drain; cool. Cut in half across the "equator" and remove any seeds. In a food processor, process orange, including skin, until it becomes a very fine puree.

Blend **4 Tbs.** orange puree, eggs, yogurt, vanilla, honey, and raisins or dates.

Combine coconut flour, cinnamon, nutmeg, cloves, salt, and baking soda. Whisk into wet ingredients until there are no more lumps. Fold in orange zest and pecans.

Divide between 12 paper lined muffin cups **or** well oiled donut shapes **or** place one tablespoon of batter into each of 48 well oiled mini muffin cups. Bake at 325° for 18-20 minutes or until a toothpick inserted in the center comes out clean.

Top with Buttercream Icing, left, and sprinkle with orange zest and chopped pecans, if you'd like.

Buttercream Icing

Beat until fluffy:
¾ c. palm shortening
¼ c. softened butter*
½ c. honey
1½ tsp. vanilla*

Note: We found palm shortening at Sprouts. This buttercream icing is so light and fluffy!

Blueberry Streusel Muffins

Makes 6 muffins

Using coconut flour, these muffins puff up nicely and make a great addition to a special brunch. Our non-SCD tasters thought these muffins were fantastic!

- 3 Tbs. coconut oil or butter*, melted
- 3 eggs
- 4 Tbs. honey
- ¼ tsp. salt
- 1 tsp. vanilla*
- ¼ tsp. almond extract*
- ¼ c. lightly stirred coconut flour
- ¼ tsp. baking soda
- 6 Tbs. frozen blueberries
- **Streusel mixture (right)**

Prepare six muffin cups by lining them with paper liners or generously greasing them with butter or coconut oil.

Blend together coconut oil or butter, eggs, honey, salt, vanilla, and almond extract. In a measuring cup, combine coconut flour and baking soda. Thoroughly mix flour mixture into egg mixture until there are no lumps.

Divide batter between six prepared muffin cups. Sprinkle 1 Tbs. blueberries on each muffin. Top each muffin with 1/6 of the streusel mixture. Bake at 400° for 15-18 minutes, or until a toothpick inserted comes out clean and muffins are golden brown.

For Streusel:

Combine with fingers, breaking up as you mix.

- 2 Tbs. unsweetened shredded coconut
- 4 Tbs. almond flour
- 6 Tbs. toasted sliced almonds
- 1 Tbs. butter*
- 1 Tbs. honey
- ½ tsp. cinnamon

*See page 7 for an explanation of what makes this ingredient legal for the Specific Carbohydrate Diet.

Food With Friends

Background credit: FreePik

Group Meals

Introduction, 59

Spaghetti Squash & Baked Potato Bar, 60

Make Your Own Pizza Bar, 64

Breakfast Board for a Group, 68

Holiday Buffet Trays, 72

Polynesian Pile On Bar, 74

Pork Pozole Soup Bar, 76

Spaghetti & Meatball Bar, 78

Taco Salad Bar, 82

Tailgate Party, 84

Tea Party, 93

Something for everyone at your table!

Background credit: FreePik

Introduction

Food with friends and family often means catering to different diets! One friend is a vegetarian, one can't eat corn, another is allergic to eggs, and your sister mustn't eat dairy. And you're on the SCD! What to do?

We meet with a group for dinner once a month and have different diets represented, so I've hit on some meals that provide something for everyone in our group and I'll share them with you here! Everyone will love them! If you want the meal to be potluck, you can prepare the main items and have guests bring components, such as freshly grated cheese, chopped tomatoes, sliced green onions, a bottle of non-SCD salsa, pepperoni slices, etc.

Getting together with friends is so enriching and there's no need to let diet issues stop you! It might mean you're doing more of the cooking, but it's worth it for the fun of bringing people together. I hope this section will help you create some delicious group meals and some welcoming moments.

Baked Potato & Spaghetti Squash Bar

Serves 12

We served this meal to people on different diets with a Kale, Fruit, & Pecan Salad, p. 63. You could have your guests bring desserts if you'd like, then add your own plate of dates stuffed with walnut halves for a sweet SCD dessert.

Note: With baked potatoes for the non-SCDers, you'll be surprised how many people will try the spaghetti squash anyway! Plan a few extra pieces, just in case.

9-10 baking potatoes for non-SCDers, scrubbed and pricked
2-3 spaghetti squash, cut and seeded
1 recipe Terrific Chili, No Beans, p. 62
¾ lb. Cheddar cheese*, freshly grated
2 bunches green onions, sliced
2 bunches broccoli, chopped small and lightly cooked
1 recipe Flag Salsa (left) and opt. bottled salsa for non-SCDers
1 carton sour cream and/or fat free sour cream for non-SCDers
1 c. homemade yogurt*
butter*

(Optional)
2-3 onions, caramelized, p. 47
avocado
sautéed mushrooms
1 lb. bacon, cooked crisp and crushed
3.8 oz. can sliced black olives
chopped tomatoes
pesto, p. 174
olive tapenade, p. 175

Flag Salsa
Makes 3½ cups

3 large firm tomatoes, diced
¼ c. chopped cilantro
2 Tbs. fresh lime juice
½ c. chopped green onion
1 to 3 jalapenos, minced (wear gloves)
Salt to taste

Combine and serve.

The day before, cut up the spaghetti squash; cut off the very tops and bottoms of the squash. Stand them on end and slice through from top to bottom to divide them in half. Remove seeds. Very large ones could be quartered. Wash and prick the potatoes, make the chili and pesto, grate the cheese, slice the green onions, and make the salsa. If using, sauté the onions, and chop the broccoli. Chill all but potatoes overnight.

On the day of your meal, bake the potatoes at 400° for 1 hour, until soft when pierced. Remove and cover with a towel to keep warm.

Meanwhile, fill a large pot with water and bring to a boil. Drop two squash halves into the water and boil for 11-12 minutes or until strands can be loosened with a fork but outside shell is still firm. Remove with large tongs and turn upside down to drain and retain heat. Continue with remaining squash halves. Fluff the interiors with a fork to make the insides spaghetti-like. Sauté the mushrooms, warm up the chili, and lightly cook the broccoli. Cut open and pinch the potatoes.

Set up your buffet with plates, potatoes, squash halves and small bowls containing all the items people can add, placing little signs if necessary to identify the item. Everyone can please themselves by piling on the things that work for their diet!

Make signs on chalk boards from a craft store.

See page 7 for an explanation of what makes this ingredient legal for the Specific Carbohydrate Diet.

Food With Friends

Terrific Chili, No Beans

Serves 6

Make this smaller recipe for your buffet because it will be eaten as a topping rather than a main dish. Leftovers are great the next day.

1 pound lean ground turkey*, chicken*, or beef
1 c. chopped onion
1 c. chopped green bell pepper
2 tsp. minced garlic
8 medium tomatoes, chopped
2 c. tomato juice*
2-3 Anaheim chilies, roasted and diced - see instructions, left
   (or use 1 small can diced green chilies*)
2 Tbs. honey
1 Tbs. dried parsley flakes
1 Tbs. ground cumin
3 tsp. smoked paprika
2 tsp. dried oregano
1½ tsp. pepper
1 tsp. salt

In a large pot, cook the meat, onion, green pepper, and garlic over medium heat until meat is no longer pink; drain. Stir in tomatoes and all other remaining ingredients. Bring to a boil. Reduce heat; cover and simmer for 25 minutes.

To Roast Chilies:*

Preheat oven to 425°. Place chilies on a foil lined, greased, baking sheet. Roast peppers until skins are beginning to blister and char, about 25 minutes. Remove from oven and gather foil around chilies while they cool. Remove seeds, membranes, and skin. Use as directed.

*See page 7 for an explanation of what makes this ingredient legal for the Specific Carbohydrate Diet.

Kale, Apple, Orange, & Pecan Salad

Serves 10-12

Massaging the dressing into the kale softens it; allowing it to mellow and soften in the fridge for a little while allows the acids, oil, and salt to work their magic.

10 oz. bag cut and cleaned kale
1 bag angel hair cabbage
2 red apples, diced
1 orange, diced
3 ribs celery, thinly sliced
½ c. pecans, toasted

For Dressing:
5 Tbs. olive oil
3 Tbs. fresh lemon or lime juice
1 tsp. prepared mustard*
1½ tsp. honey
salt

Pour kale into a large bowl; lightly salt (salt will help cut the bitter flavor). This step makes all the difference; reach into the bowl with clean hands and massage the salted kale, removing any ribs and tearing up large pieces as you massage it.

Onto the kale, drizzle olive oil, lemon juice, mustard, and honey. Massage it into the kale. Allow kale to rest for 10 minutes to a few hours. At this point you can also prepare the fruit and celery ingredients and refrigerate in a bag for later. To assemble salad, toss kale together with the bag of angel hair cabbage, the fruit, celery, and the pecans.

Note: To toast pecans, stir constantly in a dry skillet over medium heat until fragrant and beginning to brown.

"This dinner was one of the most delicious and healthiest we've tasted recently. We are glad we did not miss it." J.J.

Food With Friends

Pizza Making Party

Serves 12

Pizza making is a fun event for people on various diets! Think ahead for this meal and be freezing extra cooked chicken, cooked ground beef, grated cheese, homemade pesto, marinara, etc., so you can pull it together more quickly. The day of your dinner, make the Garlic Cheese Pizza Crusts, p. 42, and slice the fresh stuff. Serve with a big green salad! See our recipe for Herbed Yogurt Ranch Dressing, p. 66, for a delicious dressing.

Note: Set up your pizza-making station with the Naan breads and Mozzarella cheese on one side, all the other toppings in the middle, and the Garlic Pizza Crusts and Jack cheese on the other side, to avoid contamination.

Choose some or all of these pizza toppers.

See page 7 for an explanation of what makes this ingredient legal for the Specific Carbohydrate Diet.

2-4 Garlic Cheese Pizza Crusts, p. 42
10-12 Naan breads or other flatbreads for non-SCDers
homemade Marinara sauce, p. 67
homemade pesto, p. 174
2 lb. Freshly grated Monterey Jack cheese*
1 lb. grated Mozzarella cheese for non-SCDers (label clearly)
4 c. cooked and torn chicken
3 c. cooked ground beef, seasoned with basil, garlic & salt
small turkey or regular pepperoni slices for non-SCDers
4 tomatoes, sliced very thin
two 3.8-oz. cans sliced black olives*
one 8-oz. pkg. sliced mushrooms
canned or frozen artichoke hearts (boiled 5-8 minutes), roughly chopped*
½ large red onion, very thinly sliced
1 red bell pepper, chopped
2 c. fresh pineapple, chopped

parchment to go under each to prevent contamination and make it easier to work
several baking sheets

Preheat oven to 425°. Each person places their own kind of crust on a piece of parchment paper and loads on their favorite toppings. Lift the paper and loaded crusts onto sheet pans and bake for 8-12 minutes, or until cheese is bubbly. Remove and the next person can repeat, until all pizzas are cooked. Two may fit on one pan.

Group Meals

Make-Your-Own-Pizza Night is Fun!

Our table included pizza crusts, cheeses, and toppings for everyone - non-SCDers included! People enjoyed choosing from the many toppings and creating their own pizza. This was a fun and interactive meal.

Background credit: FreePik

Herbed Yogurt Ranch Dressing

Makes about 2 cups

Enjoy this thick and tasty ranch dressing on a green salad at your pizza party!

    2 c. homemade yogurt*
    ¼ c. freshly grated Parmesan cheese
    2 green onions, minced
    2 Tbs. minced fresh parsley
    1½ tsp. crushed garlic
    1 tsp. lemon zest + 2 Tbs. lemon juice
    ½ tsp. black pepper
    ½ tsp. granulated onion*
    ½ tsp. kosher salt + more to taste
    ½ tsp. dry dill or to taste
    1 Tbs. homemade mayonnaise*

Combine all ingredients and allow to chill for an hour before serving, to blend flavors.

*See page 7 for an explanation of what makes this ingredient legal for the Specific Carbohydrate Diet.

We included two types of dressings for our SCD and non-SCD guests.

Easy Marinara Sauce

Makes about 6 cups

    2 Tbs. butter*
    1 large onion, finely chopped
    2 cloves garlic, minced
    4 c. diced tomatoes (4-6 large tomatoes)
    1 carrot, grated then chopped
    2 c. tomato juice*
    1 tsp. *each;* **dry basil, oregano leaves, and salt**

In a large pot over medium heat, melt butter. Add onion and garlic; cook, stirring, until onion is limp, about 5 minutes. Add tomatoes, carrot, tomato juice, basil, oregano, and salt; stir to combine. Boil; reduce heat and simmer, uncovered, stirring occasionally, for 25-30 minutes or until sauce is thickened and much of the liquid has evaporated. You can use an immersion blender if you like smooth sauce.

Note: Serve the food with beverages and you have the perfect, friendly breakfast for 6 to 8 people. Place SCD breads and the donuts in separate parchment "boats" to avoid contamination.

Breakfast Board Quiches

Serves 6-8

Maybe you have guests staying with you or you want to have a birthday brunch! A breakfast board is a great way to provide a fun breakfast for everyone!

Follow the example of Sandy, from ReluctantEntertainer, and grab a giant wood board or platter or tray and fill it up with breakfast food like these Bacon & Egg Quiches, Cinnamon Rolls, following, sliced Best Banana Nut Bread, p. 38, and fresh fruit. Pick up a few breakfast pastries or donuts for the non-SCDers. Arrange the breads and fruit, and leave a third of the space for the quiches. Pile them on a bed of parsley after they come out of the oven, to finish off the board.

Bacon & Egg Quiches

Makes 12

Plan to pull the quiches from the oven about 10 minutes before serving.

- **12 precooked bacon strips (we use Costco's)**
- **¾ c. shredded white Cheddar cheese***
- **2 green onions, thinly sliced**
- **1½ c. finely chopped fresh spinach**
- **8 eggs**
- **1/3 c. almond milk*** *or* **3 Tbs. yogurt* mixed with water to = 1/3 c.**
- **salt and pepper to taste**
- **½ tsp. dried basil**
- **3 Roma tomatoes, cut into 12 thick slices**

Oil 12 muffin cups. Microwave the pre-cooked bacon on a paper towel, about 6 pieces at a time, for 30 seconds. You don't want the bacon crisp.

Wrap one slice of bacon around the inside of each muffin cup. Divide grated cheese, green onion, and spinach between the cups. In a large measuring cup, whisk together the eggs, almond milk or yogurt mixture, salt, pepper, and dried basil. Place muffin tin on a baking sheet; divide the egg mixture between the cups. Cover; chill a few hours or overnight.

Preheat oven to 375°. Uncover the muffin cups and top with slices of Roma tomato. Bake for 25 minutes or until eggs are puffy. Do not overbake. Allow to cool for 5 minutes before serving. Loosen sides with a knife, then remove quiches with the help of a rubber spatula.

Group Meals

Breakfast Board for a Spring Birthday

*See page 7 for an explanation of what makes this ingredient legal for the Specific Carbohydrate Diet.

My mom turned 91 this year and eats gluten-free, so this was the perfect menu for her family birthday brunch!

Background credit: FreePik

Cinnamon Rolls

Puffy and gooey, these ring all the right bells for a cinnamon roll! When I sent the recipe to Erin, she had some in the oven within 15 minutes and enjoyed every bite!

Makes 12

1½ c. almond flour
1 tsp. *each;* baking soda & coconut flour
½ tsp. cinnamon
1½ c. freshly grated Monterey Jack cheese*, lightly compressed
2 Tbs. butter*
1 Tbs. honey
1 egg, beaten with a fork
2 tsp. vanilla*

Filling
4 Tbs. softened butter*
4 tsp. cinnamon
½ c. honey + more for garnish
3 Medjool dates, diced small, or ¼ c.
1 c. finely chopped walnuts or pecans + more for garnish

Helpful Tips:

Too much cheese will make a dough that's too soft. Lightly compressing the cheese insures a true measure.

Adding the egg quickly and vigorously keeps it from turning into scrambled eggs!

Kneading the dough in a little coconut flour helps give the rolls their good texture.

See tip on bottom right, p. 71, for how to create the gooiest rolls.

Preheat oven to 375°. Combine almond flour, baking soda, coconut flour, and cinnamon; stir to remove all lumps. Set aside. Place a piece of parchment on a baking sheet; sprinkle on about 2 tsp. of **coconut flour**.

Stir filling ingredients together; set aside.

Combine cheese, butter, and honey in a large saucepan. Heat over high heat for 1+ minutes, stirring constantly, just until melted. Stir 10 to 15 times to cool slightly; vigorously stir in the egg to keep it from cooking when it touches the warm cheese. Add vanilla, then almond flour mixture, stirring until dough forms a ball and pulls away from the sides.

Turn dough out onto floured parchment covered sheet pan and knead a few times. Cover dough with another piece of parchment and roll to a 9x13-inch rectangle about ½-inch thick. Remove top parchment; distribute filling over dough. Starting on the long side, roll dough, pinching final edges together; slice into 12 pieces and place cut side up on parchment covered sheet pan or in a buttered baking dish. Press slightly to flatten. Bake for 8 minutes, turn pan, then bake 3-5 more minutes or until brown and firm. Drizzle baked rolls with **additional honey** and sprinkle with **nuts**.

*See page 7 for an explanation of what makes this ingredient legal for the Specific Carbohydrate Diet.

Food With Friends

Holiday Open House Do-It-Yourself Buffet Trays

Serves 24

Make sure most of the food at your buffet is SCD compliant! This year, when you gather friends and family for an open house, office party, or any other holiday get-together, use these ideas to provide more food and greater variety than prepared party trays. These will include mostly legal meats, breads, p. 35, cheeses, and salads, along with deli meats, breads and maybe a potato salad for non-SCDers. Beverages could include an iced coffee station with legal options, and apple cider for all.

Tzatziki Dip

2 c. homemade yogurt, dripped overnight*
1 small cucumber, peeled, seeded, shredded, and drained 30 minutes
½ c. green onions, sliced
½ tsp. *each;* salt, honey
1 tsp. cumin
1-2 drops hot pepper sauce*

Combine yogurt, cucumber, onions, salt, honey, cumin, and pepper sauce. Stir before serving.

Meat & Sandwich Platter

- **6 boneless chicken breasts, poached and sliced**
- **1 Tri-Tip beef roast, 2½ to 4 pounds (right)**
- **Rosemary Meatballs (right)**
- **homemade mayonnaise*, p. 176**
- **prepared mustard***
- **2 heads butter lettuce leaves for wrapping, more for garnish**
- **Grain-Free Focaccia or other choice from our bread section, p. 35**
- assorted breads for sandwiches for non-SCDers
- ½ pound *each;* deli ham and sliced turkey for non-SCDers
- 1 pound sliced salami for non-SCDers

Cook and freeze chicken, roast, and meatballs in advance. On the party day, thaw and arrange attractively on a lettuce lined platter; keep SCD choices all in one area. Pile meatballs in a footed dish in the center. Separate legal and non-SCD breads in separate baskets on the side.

Buffet Menu
Sliced Meats
Lettuce Wrappers
Breads
Veggie Tray
SunDriedTomato Dip
Tzatziki Dip
Fresh Fruit Chunks
Various Cheeses
Olives
Spiced Nuts, p. 90
Cole Slaw, p. 88
Beverage Station

Tzatziki Dip

Rosemary Meatballs

Makes 32 meatballs

Moist and tasty, dip them in either of the dips and add them to your buffet.

1 pound lean ground beef or turkey*
1 medium onion, grated
4-5 small sprigs fresh rosemary
Salt & pepper

Combine meat and grated onion in a bowl. Mince rosemary leaves to get 2 tsp. Add to the meat. Add a scant 1 tsp. salt and ½ tsp. pepper. Mix thoroughly.

Divide mixture into quarters. Make each quarter into 8 meatballs. Heat nonstick skillet over high heat; cook meatballs in batches for 2 minutes. Reduce heat and roll meatballs so they don't stick. Cook, turning occasionally, until just firm, 3 to 4 more minutes. Don't overcook. Cool, then freeze, tightly wrapped, if made ahead. Serve warm, garnished with rosemary sprigs.

Oven Roasted Tri-Tip Beef Roast

To prepare for your buffet trays, cook beef roast ahead of time, slice with an electric knife, arrange attractively, and freeze. Thaw on the morning of your party.

1 tri-tip beef roast, 2½ to 4 pounds
Spice Rub (right)

Preheat oven to 450°. If you get an untrimmed roast, slash fat on top in 3 or 4 places, trying not to cut meat. Rub all over with spice rub.

Place meat in a rack in a pan and place in preheated oven for 15 minutes ONLY. Turn oven down to 225° and continue roasting for a total of 45 minutes *per pound*, including the first 15 minutes. So a 2½ pound tri-tip should roast for about 1 hour and 50 minutes, total time. Internal temp should be 130° for rare/medium or 150° to 160° for medium well. Tri-Tip is quite lean so is ideally cooked to no more than medium.

*See page 7 for an explanation of what makes this ingredient legal for the SCD.

Sun Dried Tomato Dip

2 c. homemade yogurt, dripped overnight*
½ c. sun dried tomatoes
½ c. fresh basil leaves
1 Tbs. olive oil
½ tsp. crushed garlic
1 tsp. honey
Salt & pepper to taste

Place dried tomatoes in a small saucepan and cover with water. Simmer; remove from heat; set aside to plump for 20 minutes. Drain.

In a food processor, puree tomatoes, basil, oil, garlic, and honey. Salt & pepper to taste. Fold tomato puree into yogurt and thoroughly combine. Chill. May be made up to 3 days ahead.

Spice Rub

1 Tbs. cumin
1 Tbs. olive oil
¾ tsp. minced garlic
1 tsp. ground coriander
½ tsp. paprika
¼ tsp. cayenne pepper
Salt & pepper to taste

Combine. Use this amount for a smaller roast and **double** for a larger roast.

Food With Friends

Polynesian Pile On
Serves 12

This is one of our favorite group meals. We also love to take it along when we're camping. When friends of ours were in Bali, they were served this same meal, with servers coming around and graciously offering each individual item for people to add to their "stack" if they wanted it. It is a fun, delicious, and complete meal for everyone.

Curry Powder Recipe

Combine in a small labeled jar and use as directed.

4 tsp. cumin
4 tsp. coriander
4 tsp. turmeric
1 tsp. cinnamon
½ tsp. nutmeg
½ tsp. cayenne pepper
½ tsp. black pepper
½ tsp. cloves
½ tsp. cardamom

*See page 7 for an explanation of what makes this ingredient legal for the Specific Carbohydrate Diet.

- **1 head cauliflower, made into cauliflower rice and lightly cooked with lime zest, green onion, and lime juice**
- **6 c. cooked rice, for non-SCDers (we added lime here, too)**
- **2 whole chickens, cooked, meat removed (save and freeze broth for another meal)**
- **2-3 pkg. chicken gravy mix, prepared with added 1+ tsp. regular curry powder, for non-SCDers**
- **½ c. SCD yogurt* per SCDer, mixed with homemade curry powder* (left), crushed pineapple,* and salt, at room temp.**
- **1 lb. freshly grated Cheddar cheese***
- **1 c. sliced green onions**
- **2 c. celery, finely chopped**
- **2 c. sliced almonds**
- **4 c. crushed pineapple***
- **2 c. unsweetened coconut, sweetened to taste with honey**
- **1 pkg. or can of chow mien noodles for non-SCDers**

To serve, set up a line with plates and ask people to layer items in order; hot rice or cauliflower rice, chicken pieces, topping with gravy or yogurt mixture. Then layer on cheese, green onions, celery, almonds, pineapple, coconut, and other toppings, according to what each person eats. Eat down through the stack to get the full flavor.

Polynesian Pile On

Polynesian Pile On is a great meal for kids and adults alike. Everyone can take what they like and what suits their diet.

We love to serve Polynesian Pile On at camp.

Background credit: FreePik

Pork Pozole Soup Bar

Serves 12

While this soup won't work for your vegetarian friends, they could make a salad out of the toppings if you add black beans for non-SCDers and a dressing, so there's still something for everyone. You start with a flavorful pork soup and add all kinds of things to personalize it! Many families use this type of recipe to "clean out the fridge" at the end of the week, so feel free to be creative.

3 pounds pork tenderloin, trimmed and cut into bite-sized pieces
8 garlic cloves, minced
10-12 tsp. homemade Taco Seasoning Mix (left)
2 16-oz. packages frozen baby lima beans
10 c. diced tomatoes (about 10-12 Roma tomatoes)
6 c. tomato juice*
1 c. chopped fresh cilantro

Taco Seasoning Mix

Combine in a small labeled jar and use as directed.

6 Tbs. sweet paprika
8 tsp. ground cumin
4 Tbs. dried oregano
1 tsp. cayenne pepper
4 tsp. parsley flakes, crushed
2 tsp. granulated garlic*
2 tsp. dried, granulated onion*

Set out Bowls of Toppings:
- finely shredded lettuce (provide more if a vegetarian will be making a salad)
- sliced radishes
- sliced green onions
- diced avocado
- freshly grated Cheddar* or Monterey Jack cheese*
- hard cooked eggs, quartered
- cilantro, chopped
- lime wedges to squeeze
- diced red onion
- homemade yogurt*, and/or sour cream for non-SCDers
- tortilla chips for non-SCDers

Heat a large, oiled soup pan over medium-high heat. Sprinkle pork with Mexican Spice Mix; add pork and garlic to pan; cook 4 to 6 minutes or until richly browned. Stir in limas, tomatoes, tomato juice, 2 tsp. **salt**, and **3 cups water**. Bring to a boil; cover, reduce heat; simmer 20 minutes or until pork is tender. Stir in cilantro. Serve with toppings.

Pork Pozole Soup Bar

Background credit: FreePik

Food With Friends

Spaghetti and Meatball Bar
Serves 12

Note: Cook more spaghetti squash than you think you need in case a "regular" eater decides to try it out!

The Marinara sauce can be made ahead and frozen, and so can the meatballs.

See page 7 for an explanation of what makes this ingredient legal for the Specific Carbohydrate Diet.

Everyone will enjoy piling the delicious sauce, meatballs, and other toppings onto their preferred base. Finish it off with a big green salad with bottled (for non-SCDers) and homemade dressing (right). Grain-Free Focaccia Bread, p. 81, with butter and Ciabatta rolls and butter for non-SCDers round out the meal.

2-3 oz. thin spaghetti <u>per non-SCDer</u> (When held in your hand it's < an inch in diameter.), or 20 to 30 oz. to serve 10

1-3 medium spaghetti squash

1-2 packages frozen spiralized vegetables

double recipe Easy Marinara Sauce, p. 67

Make-Ahead Mini Meatballs, p. 80 (2-3 per person)

1 3.8-oz. can sliced black olives*, drained

1 bag frozen artichoke hearts, simmered 5-8 minutes, drained, chopped *or* **2 cans water packed artichoke hearts*, chopped**

4 large tomatoes, diced

Basil Pesto, p. 174

2 c. freshly grated Parmesan cheese*

Aunt Trish's Dressing, right

Fill a large pot with water and bring to a boil. Cut off the very tops and bottoms of the squash. Stand them on end and slice down, from top to bottom to divide them in half. Remove seeds. Drop two squash halves at a time into the water and boil for 11-12 minutes or until strands can be loosened with a fork but outside is still firm. Remove with large tongs and turn upside down to drain and retain heat. Fluff with a fork to make the insides spaghetti-like.

Cook spaghetti and spiralized veggies according to package directions.

To assemble your food line, provide plates, cooked and drained spaghetti, fluffed spaghetti squash, cooked spiralized veggies, meatballs, hot marinara sauce, sliced olives, chopped artichoke hearts, pesto, diced tomatoes, and Parmesan. Provide bowls for the green salad with dressings nearby. Guests can top their spaghetti plate with a buttered focaccia or ciabatta roll if desired.

Group Meals

Aunt Trish's Dressing
Adapted from Pioneer Woman Magazine

½ c. olive oil
3 Tbs. freshly grated Parmesan cheese
½ tsp. salt, plus more to taste
Black pepper, to taste
¼ tsp. honey
1 to 2 dashes paprika
1/3 c. fresh lemon juice
1 whole garlic clove, peeled

Combine in a jar. Shake it up and store it in the fridge until using. To serve, remove garlic clove and shake well again, then drizzle half over salad. Season with salt and pepper. Toss well, adding more dressing if needed.

Spaghetti & Meatball Bar

Background credit: FreePik

Make Ahead Mini-Meatballs

Makes about 80 meatballs; enough for 16-20 servings

Give ground beef a gourmet flair by making a big batch of these delicious meatballs adapted from Cuisine At Home magazine. Freeze the meatballs in quart size bags of 20 each, and figure 2 to 3 meatballs for the average serving. Thaw and heat the number you need for your group, and save the rest for future meals!

8 strips bacon, diced
1 c. diced onion
4 cloves garlic, minced
3 pounds lean ground beef
1 c. almond flour
½ c. minced fresh parsley
2 tsp. *each*; **paprika and kosher salt**
1 tsp. black pepper
4 eggs, beaten

Preheat oven to 400°. Oil 4 cookie sheets. Cook bacon in a nonstick skillet over medium-high heat until crisp, about 5-6 minutes; remove and set aside on a paper towel lined plate. Pour off all but 2 Tbs. drippings from skillet.

Over medium heat, sauté onion in the bacon drippings until softened; about 3 minutes. Add garlic to skillet; cook 1 minute.

Combine beef, cooked bacon, onion mixture, almond flour, parsley, paprika, salt, and pepper in a large bowl. Stir in beaten eggs.

Form mixture into 1-inch mini meatballs and place on prepared pans. (Wetting your hands with water periodically will prevent sticking.) Bake meatballs in batches, if necessary, to prevent overcrowding, baking until fully cooked, about 10-12 minutes. Cool completely and freeze in four labeled zip-top freezer bags.

Grain-Free Focaccia Bread

Makes 16-20 squares

- 2 c. almond flour
- ¾ c. homemade yogurt*
- ½ c. freshly grated Monterey Jack cheese*
- ½ c. freshly grated Cheddar cheese*
- 1 tsp. baking soda
- ¼ tsp. salt
- ½ tsp. black pepper
- 3 eggs
- 3 Tbs. melted butter*
- 2 green onions, finely sliced

For Topping:

- ½ tsp. coarse salt
- 2 Tbs. finely grated Cheddar cheese*
- 1 Tbs. (or more) dried rosemary

Note: Enjoy this recipe, adapted from Raman Prasad's cookbook, *Recipes for the Specific Carbohydrate Diet.*

If serving breads in the same basket, separate with parchment to avoid contamination.

For additional authentic tastes, also top dough with sliced olives and a sprinkling of dried oregano leaves before baking.

*See page 7 for an explanation of what makes this ingredient legal for the Specific Carbohydrate Diet.

Preheat oven to 375°. Grease a 9x13-inch baking dish.

Make a thick stack of paper towels and pour yogurt onto it. Top with another thick stack of paper towels and press down lightly. Allow to sit for five to ten minutes, flipping once. Remove thickened yogurt with a rubber spatula.

In a food processor, combine almond flour, yogurt, Jack cheese, Cheddar cheese, baking soda, salt, pepper, eggs, melted butter, and green onion. Process until well blended. Remove from the food processor and spread into the prepared baking dish.

Combine topping ingredients; sprinkle over bread dough. Bake until brown, 25-30 minutes. Cool and cut into squares.

Food With Friends

See page 7 for an explanation of what makes this ingredient legal for the Specific Carbohydrate Diet.

Taco Salad Bar

Serves 12

Salads are wonderful for summer get-togethers and the flavorful components of this salad bar will make people happy. Relax while you munch and talk about interesting things. Serve with tea and strawberry lemonade, p. 92, like we did.

2½ pounds ground beef or turkey*, cooked and drained
3-4 c. cooked navy beans,* with some cooking liquid
Taco Seasoning Mix, p. 76
2 heads leaf lettuce, washed, drained, and chopped
1 head iceberg lettuce, washed, drained, and chopped
4 large tomatoes, diced
4 large avocados, diced
6 green onions, thinly sliced
2 small cans sliced black olives*
¾ lb. freshly grated Cheddar cheese*
½ bag frozen petite corn, thawed, for non-SCDers
1 bag regular Fritos, for non-SCDers
1 carton sour cream, for non-SCDers
1 c. homemade yogurt,* as a topper
1 recipe **Cilantro Dressing (right)**
purchased dressing for non-SCDers, if desired
lime wedges to squeeze

In a skillet, combine cooked ground meat and Taco Seasoning Mix to taste, about **8 teaspoons**. Cook, adding a little **water** to moisten. Meanwhile, gently warm beans with plenty of Taco Seasoning Mix.

Assemble your taco salad bar with plates, a large bowl of mixed lettuce, warm meat, warm beans, and individual bowls of the different toppings. Let people go around and build their own taco salad, taking whatever suits their own diet.

Okay, let's eat!

Cilantro Dressing

Makes about 2½ cups

Adapted from culinaryhill

2 c. cilantro leaves, stems cut off, compressed
1 c. homemade yogurt*
4 cloves finely minced garlic
1 Tbs. honey
¼ c. fresh lime juice
½ tsp. salt, or to taste
½ c. olive oil

In a food processor, combine and process cilantro, yogurt, minced garlic, honey, lime juice, and salt until very smooth. With the motor running, slowly add olive oil through the feed-tube to create an emulsion. Taste and correct seasonings. Pour into a serving container and chill at least 10 minutes to blend flavors.

This dressing was very popular with our tasters. They liked the deep cilantro flavor and the tartness with their taco salads.

Food With Friends

Tailgate Party

Serves 8

Home games are the perfect setting for gathering with other fans and enjoying a tailgate party before the game. Support your team and have a feast at the same time! Eat your fill as you kick back, play corn hole, throw the football, and wait for the game to start. Our menu serves 8, and has plenty of delicious food for everyone, and you can add chips and packages of cookies for the non-SCDers.

Artwork credit: PTO ClipartGallery

Tailgate Party Menu

Baked Onion Cheese Dip

Green Pork Chili Verde

Chicken Skewers with Avocado Sauce

Fresh & Fruity Coleslaw

Carrot Radish Salad

Fresh Fruit Skewers

Spiced Pecans

Fruit Cookies

Strawberry Lemonade

University of Arizona Tucson

Mizzou, University of Missouri

UCLA, From Bruins Nation

Baked Onion Cheese Dip

Makes 3 cups

Dig into this oniony delight at your tailgate picnic. Provide small paper cups so SCDers can scoop out their serving of dip, preventing it from being contaminated by people digging in with chips.

- 1 c. Monterey Jack cheese*
- 1 c. homemade yogurt, dripped overnight
- ½ c. homemade mayonnaise*, p. 176
- 1 Anaheim chile, roasted, peeled, and chopped, p. 62
    - *or* 2 Tbs. canned diced green chiles*
- ¼ tsp. dried thyme
- 2 c. chopped white onions, divided in half
- assorted dippers such as plain pork rinds and veggies and chips for non-SCDers

Note: To make wide vegetable dippers, slice large carrots and cucumbers diagonally.

Combine the cheese, yogurt, mayonnaise, green chiles, thyme, and half the onions in a food processor; process until blended. Pour into a bowl and stir in remaining onions.

Transfer to a greased 3-cup baking dish. Bake, uncovered, at 375° for 20-25 minutes, or until bubbly. Cover and keep warm until serving.

*See page 7 for an explanation of what makes this ingredient legal for the Specific Carbohydrate Diet.

Green Pork Chili Verde

Serves 8

A small amount of fat left on the meat is enough to make the meat tender and enrich the flavor of this spicy Chili Verde recipe from Everyday Food magazine. Score a touchdown when you add it to your tailgate picnic menu! Chili simmers for 2 hours and may be refrigerated for up to 3 days. Serve over plain crunchy pork rinds or corn tortilla chips for non-SCDers, if you'd like.

1 pound tomatillos (husks removed), washed
1 Tbs. olive oil
4 pounds boneless country-style pork, trimmed and cut into ½-inch chunks
coarse salt and ground pepper
4 Anaheim chiles, roasted, peeled, and chopped, p. 62 or 2 cans (4 oz. each) diced green chiles*
1 Tbs. dried oregano
1 large onion, chopped
5 garlic cloves, crushed
2 jalapeno peppers (ribs and seeds removed for less heat), finely diced (wear gloves)
1/3 c. chopped fresh cilantro, plus leaves for garnish
Cheddar cheese, freshly grated*
lime wedges

*See page 7 for an explanation of what makes this ingredient legal for the Specific Carbohydrate Diet.

In a blender or food processor, puree tomatillos until smooth; set aside.

In a non-stick skillet, heat oil over medium-high heat. Season pork with salt and pepper. Working in batches and transferring to a plate as you go, brown pork, 4 to 6 minutes per batch. Add a little water to remove browned bits.

Remove pork (and juices) to a 5-quart Dutch oven or heavy pot. Add tomatillos, green chiles, oregano, onion, garlic, jalapenos, and **1 cup water**; season with salt and pepper and stir. Bring to a boil; reduce to a simmer. Cover, and cook, stirring occasionally, until pork is tender, about 2 hours. (To store, refrigerate for up to 3 days, or freeze for up to 3 months.)

Just before serving, stir in chopped cilantro; serve chili verde with cheddar cheese and lime wedges, and garnish with cilantro leaves.

Chicken Skewers with Avocado Sauce

Makes 16 skewers

Take along your portable grill and cook these tasty skewers when you get there or do them before you leave. They are quick and easy to marinate and transport.

1 pound (2 large) boneless skinless chicken breasts
½ c. lime juice
1 Tbs. cider vinegar
1 tsp. honey
1 Tbs. tomato juice*
1 tsp. roasted Anaheim chiles*, p. 62
½ tsp. salt

Sauce:
1 medium ripe avocado, peeled and pitted
½ c. homemade yogurt*
1 tsp. honey
2 Tbs. minced fresh cilantro
2 tsp. lime juice
1 tsp. grated lime peel
¼ tsp. salt

Gently pound chicken to ¼-inch thickness; cut lengthwise into sixteen 1-in.-wide strips. In a large zip-top bag, combine the lime juice, vinegar, honey, tomato juice, chiles, and salt; add the chicken. Seal bag and turn to coat; refrigerate for at least 30 minutes.

Meanwhile, for the sauce, place sauce ingredients in a food processor; cover and process until blended. Transfer to a serving bowl; place avocado seed in sauce to help prevent browning. Cover and refrigerate, then remove seed before serving.

Drain chicken and discard marinade. Thread onto 16 metal or soaked wooden skewers. Coat grill rack with oil before starting the grill. Grill, covered, over medium heat for 4-6 minutes on each side or until no longer pink. Serve with sauce.

Food With Friends

Fresh & Fruity Coleslaw

Serves 10

A juicy, crunchy salad is perfect at a tailgate picnic!

    1 package (16 oz.) coleslaw mix
    2 celery ribs, chopped
    1 c. seedless grapes, halved
    1 medium tart apple, chopped

Dressing:
    1/3 c. homemade yogurt*
    1/3 c. fresh orange juice
    1/3 c. homemade mayonnaise*, p. 176
    1 Tbs. lemon juice
    1 Tbs. honey

In a large bowl, combine the coleslaw mix, celery, grapes, and apple. Combine the dressing ingredients; pour over the top. Toss to coat. Cover and refrigerate for at least 2 hours before serving.

Denver Bronco Tailgate Party

88

Carrot Radish Salad

Serves 8

6 c. shredded carrots
14 radishes, sliced and cut into strips
½ c. raisins
lettuce leaves, optional

Lime Vinaigrette:
4 Tbs. lime juice
4 Tbs. olive oil
1 tsp. salt
1 tsp. grated lime peel
1 tsp. honey
½ tsp. pepper

In a small bowl, combine the carrots, radishes, and raisins. In a jar with a tight-fitting lid, combine vinaigrette ingredients; shake well. Drizzle over carrot mixture and toss to coat. Serve in a lettuce-lined bowl if desired, or salad may be wrapped in lettuce to eat it.

See page 7 for an explanation of what makes this ingredient legal for the Specific Carbohydrate Diet.

Fruit Skewers

To make fruit skewers, place three pieces of fruit on each toothpick. We used fresh **pineapple chunks**, fresh **cherry halves**, and **melon cubes**. You might also choose grapes, apple pieces, or other pieces of seasonal fruit.

Spiced Pecans

Makes 5 cups

These pecans from Healthy Cooking make a yummy and slightly sweet snack. Take them to munch at the game or fill a jar as a gift for the holidays.

- **1 egg white**
- **1 pound raw pecan halves**
- **2 Tbs. honey**
- **2½ to 3 tsp. ground cinnamon**
- **½ tsp. salt**

In a large mixing bowl, beat egg white until frothy. Add pecans; stir gently to coat. Combine the honey, cinnamon, and salt; add to nut mixture and stir gently to coat.

Spread onto a large rimmed greased baking sheet. Bake, uncovered, at 325° for 20 minutes or until lightly browned, stirring once. Cool completely. Store in an airtight container.

Fruit Cookies

Our friend, Dorothy Sheldrake, created these cookies for her husband and we think you'll love them! Take them along to your tailgate party.

   44 dried apricots (whole, pitted, from Costco)
   2 c. unsalted pecans, plus more for garnish
   1 c. golden raisins
   1 Tbs. almond extract*
   2 Tbs. honey
   2 Tbs. softened or melted butter*

Grind apricots first to just about half the desired texture, then add the rest of the ingredients. Grind mixture until you have a coarse texture.

Roll into one-inch balls or use a small scoop. Place on a cookie sheet covered with parchment paper and flatten slightly. To flatten, dampen the palm of your hand so the cookie does not stick. Place half of a pecan in the center of each cookie and press just enough to make it stay.

Bake for 25 minutes at 325°.

*See page 7 for an explanation of what makes this ingredient legal for the Specific Carbohydrate Diet.

Strawberry Lemonade

Makes about 1 gallon

Adapted from Everyday Food, this refreshing pink lemonade is fun to take to a tailgate party in a big thermos or serve at a tea or summer party. The recipe may be cut in half.

In a large pot, combine 1½ c. **honey**, 3 cups sliced unsweetened (thawed if frozen) **strawberries**, 6-12 **lemons** and 1-2 **limes** (depending on how citrusy you want it), all citrus very thinly sliced. Mash with a potato masher for 5 minutes. Stir in 8 cups **water** and let sit 30 minutes. Pour through a strainer into a large container, pressing on solids to extract as much liquid as possible; discard solids. Stir in 4 cups cold **sparkling water** *or* cold water. Serve over ice.

Our tasters loved and preferred this lemonade with the full amount of citrus, but for a more standard taste, use the lower amount of citrus and additional honey, to taste. Photo is of a half recipe.

Afternoon Tea

It's fun to gather friends on a blustery day and share finger foods and hot cups of tea. I recently had a tea time with three girls and their moms. Schedules lined up and we threw it together for the following Saturday! Being last minute made it better… I started with low expectations, a few things already in the freezer, and went from there.

Tea for SCDers is totally possible! This menu will be good for anyone, making sure to check for nut and egg allergies.

Create your menu from choices on the following pages. Depending on the number of people, choose 3 or 4 items from Sandwiches & Savories (non-sweet), 2 to 3 from Neutral Items, and 2 or 3 Sweets. Check our Appetizers, p. 15, for more ideas.

Food With Friends

Good food and conversation make the perfect setting for Tea, but if you have pretty dishes or cups, this is the time to pull them out! Snipping some pretty flowers or greens from your yard will set the tone for a beautiful time together. But remember, people are more important than things!

At our tea, an old satin purse was filled with various questions. Each person found one they liked, then each talked a bit about theirs. We learned that one girl, if she could become an animal, would choose to be a horse or a monkey, a mom told about train trips taken with her grandma, and a fifth grader told about her teacher, who is helpful and encouraging. Another shared her families' Christmas tradition of hiding a blanched almond in porridge, with the finder winning a prize! As everyone put on their coats and rain boots to leave, there was laughing, talking, and gladness that we'd spent two hours together.

Sandwiches & Savories for Tea
(choose 3 or 4)

- **Best Banana Nut Bread sandwiches, p. 38, with either butter or peanut butter* spread between two thin slices (or Nutella for the non-SCDers)**
- **Thai Chicken Satay Skewers, p. 21**
- **Amaretto Apricots, p. 17**
- **Bacon Wrapped Dates, p. 18**
- **Deviled Eggs, p. 102**
- **Egg salad made with homemade mayo, p. 176 on Focaccia squares, p. 81, or on large cucumber slices, or regular bread circles for non-SCDers**
- **Camembert Popovers, p. 100**
- **Cheese cubes**

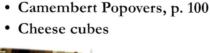

Neutral Tea Items
(choose 2 or 3)
- Apple Ginger Spice Scones, p. 36
- Fruit skewers, p. 90
- Whole strawberries
- Small bunches of sweet grapes
- Baby carrots and other cut up veggies

Sweets for Tea
(choose 2 or 3)
- Coconut Almond Biscotti, p. 184
- Lemon Cookies, p. 185
- Cookie Press Cookies, p. 152
- Peanut Butter Cookies, p. 153
- Mini Almond Grape Cakes, p. 141
- Western Fruit Cake, p. 140
- Mini Muffins, p. 52 and following
- English Toffee, p. 159
- Sugar Plums, p. 161
- Watermelon Jello Dessert jelled in individual tea cups, p. 159

- Steaming hot spearmint and/or black tea
- Homemade Strawberry Lemonade, p. 92

Food With Friends

Main Dish Tapas

What Are Tapas?, 98

Mahi-Mahi & Bacon Skewers, 99

Camembert Popovers, 100

Chile Cheese Squares, 101

Ten Deviled Eggs, 102

Oven Baked Tortilla, 103

Spinach Mushroom Tortilla, 104

Chicken Salad With Raisins, 105

Tasty Chicken Wings with Sauces, 106

Asian Lettuce Wraps, 108

Chicken in Lemon & Garlic, 109

Chicken & Olive Roll-ups, 110

Porterhouse Steak with Garlic, 111

Paprika Spareribs, 112

Mini Pork Brochettes, 112

Spanish Meatballs, 113

Falafel with Cucumber Salad, 114

Food With Friends

What Are Tapas?

Have you heard of tapas? Pronounced *"top'-us,"* they're small servings of food that you can mostly eat with your fingers, and they're becoming more known and enjoyed in the U.S.! Tapas originated in Spain, where people can go into a tapas bar and choose from plates piled high with delicious and varied tapas, just remembering what they ate and paying by trust at the end of the evening, a system that works well.

The word "tapas" originated with a word that means "covering," and people think little servings of bread or meat were offered to "cover" the glass of beer to keep out gnats and flies and to have something to nibble. It grew from there and now people like to go in with friends and family, spend the evening, and make a meal of all the different tapas choices.

BlogFuerteHoteles

We have a popular tapas restaurant in our town where you come in and they bring small plates and forks for each person and little dishes of roasted almonds and mixed olives for you to munch while you order. You choose four or five small plates which they bring out as they're ready, and you sit and enjoy tasting, not knowing what will come next. If you're still hungry, you can order more and the meal can take most of the evening if you want.

Tapas dining lends itself so well to special diets such as the SCD because the selections are dense with meats, fish, eggs, nuts, cheese, olives, dried fruits, and salads. They're also perfect because people can reach and take what they want with no focus on what you're not eating. I think you're going to enjoy gathering with some friends and trying out a few delicious tapas at home! While our recipes aren't all strictly what you'd find in Spain, they fit the idea of small servings that can be mostly eaten with your fingers. Take a look at our appetizer recipes as well! I hope you enjoy trying these recipes and this new style of eating and entertaining!

From Barcelona-Home.com
Photo credit: Getty Images
Tapas-NotesFromSpain.com

Mahi-Mahi & Bacon Skewers

Serves 6-8 for tapas

These flavorful skewers are fun to eat and taste great.

- 9 oz. mahi-mahi filet, 1-inch thick or swordfish filet
- 12 fresh rosemary stems
- 4 Tbs. olive oil
- juice of 1 small lemon
- 1 garlic clove, crushed
- 6 thick meaty bacon slices
- salt and pepper
- lemon wedges to garnish
- Garlic aioli (recipe below)

Cut filet into 24 fairly equal cubes; set aside. To prepare rosemary skewers, strip leaves off bottom half of stems and set aside, leaving some leaves at one end.

For marinade, finely chop a few reserved rosemary leaves (makes 1 Tbs.) and whisk with oil, lemon juice, garlic, and salt and pepper to taste in a non-metallic bowl. Reserve a few tablespoons of marinade for basting. Add fish pieces to remaining marinade and toss until coated. Cover and let marinate in the refrigerator for 1-2 hours. Make Garlic Aioli; refrigerate.

Partially pre-cook bacon, then cut each slice in half lengthwise, then in half widthwise; roll up each piece. Thread 2 fish pieces alternately with 2 bacon rolls onto the prepared rosemary skewers. Use a metal skewer to pierce the bacon if necessary.

Preheat the broiler, grill pan, or BBQ. If you are cooking under a broiler, arrange skewers on the broiler rack so leaves protrude from the broiler and therefore do not catch fire during cooking. Cook skewers on medium heat, turning gently and basting with reserved marinade, for 10 minutes, or until cooked. Served hot, garnished with lemons and aioli.

Garlic Aioli

Makes 1 cup

- ¾ c. homemade mayonnaise*
- 3 cloves garlic, minced
- 1½ Tbs. lemon juice
- ½ tsp. *each;* salt & pepper

Combine ingredients in a bowl. Cover and refrigerate for at least 30 minutes before serving.

*See page 7 for an explanation of what makes this ingredient legal for the Specific Carbohydrate Diet.

Background credit: FreePik

Camembert Popovers

Makes 24

These bite-size puffs deflate and act as warm pillows for tomato tapenade, below, or olive tapenade (p. 175) and are perfect to serve as a protein filled tapas snack or at a tea. Recipe comes from Rozanne Gold's "Low Carb 1-2-3" cookbook.

**8 ounces Camembert or Brie cheese*, chilled
3 extra-large eggs
½ c. tomato tapenade (below) or salmon caviar**

Using a small, sharp knife, cut the rind from the cold cheese (if using Camembert), and discard the rind. (Brie's rind is meant to be eaten.) Let the cheese sit at room temperature for 30 minutes.

Preheat the oven to 350°. In a food processor, place the eggs and process briefly. Slice cheese into 1-inch pieces and add them to the processor. Process until very smooth and thick, about 1 minute.

Coat two 12-hole mini-muffin tins (about 1¼" in diameter) with oil. Spoon 1 tablespoon of the cheese mixture into each cup. Bake for 13 to 15 minutes, until the popovers are slightly golden, puffed, and just firm to the touch. Remove the tins from the oven, let them sit for 1 minute, then remove the popovers by turning the muffin tins over and using a knife, if necessary. Top each warm or room-temperature popover patty with a dollop of tomato or olive tapenade or caviar and serve.

Tomato Tapenade

½ c. pitted black olives
2 tsp. fresh rosemary, chopped
2 tsp. fresh oregano, chopped
4 garlic cloves, minced
2½ pounds Roma tomatoes, halved & seeded
2 Tbs. olive oil
¼ tsp. pepper

Combine olives, herbs, garlic, and tomatoes on an oiled baking sheet, tomatoes cut side up. Bake at 300° for 2 hours and 15 minutes. Cool and chop in a food processor. Stir in pepper.

Chile Cheese Squares

Makes 24 squares

My friend serves these squares as a main dish for dinner and her family can't get enough of them. We love to serve them for brunch or an occasion when finger food is what you want, such as a tapas party or Christmas buffet.

10 eggs
½ c. almond flour
½ tsp. baking soda
½ tsp. salt
4 Anaheim chilies, roasted, p. 62 *or* one 7-oz. and one 4-oz. can diced mild green chiles*, undrained
2 c. homemade yogurt*
1 lb. grated Monterey Jack cheese*, freshly grated
½ c. butter*, melted

Preheat oven to 400°. In a large bowl, beat eggs with an electric mixer until completely mixed. Add almond flour, baking soda, and salt, beating until incorporated. Beat in green chiles and yogurt. Stir in cheese and melted butter.

Pour egg mixture into an oiled 9 x 13 inch pan. Bake at 400° for 15 minutes; reduce heat to 350° and bake for 30 to 35 minutes, until brown on top. Cool slightly and cut into 24 squares.

*See page 7 for an explanation of what makes this ingredient legal for the Specific Carbohydrate Diet.

Ten Kinds of Deviled Eggs!

Each recipe fills 12 halves

Recipes are adapted from Healthy Cooking Magazine and Food Network.com.

Cut 6 peeled hard-cooked eggs in half lengthwise. Remove yolks; set aside egg whites. Mash yolks; stir in 3 Tbs. mayonnaise*, 1/8 t. *each* salt and pepper and one of the combinations below. Pile mixture into egg whites and garnish. Each recipe fills 12 halves.

Mexican: 3 Tbs. leftover homemade salsa, p. 60, ¼ tsp. ground cumin. Garnish with fresh jalapeno slices and dust with paprika.

Italian: ½ tsp. dried basil, ½ tsp. dried oregano. Garnish with freshly grated Parmesan cheese* and fresh parsley.

Guacamole: ¼ small avocado, mashed, 2 cherry tomatoes, finely chopped, ½ tsp. lime zest, 1 tsp. lime juice. 1 drop hot sauce*.

Buffalo: 2 Tbs. crumbled Blue cheese*, 1 Tbs. finely chopped celery, ¼ tsp. hot pepper sauce*. Garnish with celery leaves.

Greek #1: 2 Tbs. crumbled Blue cheese*, 1 tsp. dried oregano, ½ tsp. grated lemon peel, ½ tsp. lemon juice. Garnish with black olive pieces.

Greek #2: 2 Tbs. homemade yogurt*, 1 tsp. prepared mustard,* ½ tsp. dried parsley, ½ tsp. dried mint, 1/8 tsp. crushed garlic, 2 Tbs. finely chopped cucumber, 1 tsp. lemon juice. Garnish with a piece of sliced cucumber.

Herbed Eggs: 2 Tbs. homemade yogurt*, 1 tsp. prepared mustard*, ½ tsp. dried parsley, 1/8 tsp. crushed garlic. Garnish with paprika and a parsley leaf.

Bacon Cheddar: 1 bacon strip, cooked crisp and crumbled, 1 Tbs. finely shredded Cheddar cheese*, ½ tsp. prepared mustard*, ½ tsp. honey, pinch pepper. Garnish with a sprinkle of paprika and a few pieces of grated cheese.

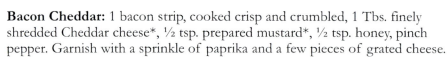

BLT: 1 Tbs. homemade mayonnaise*, 3 slices bacon cooked crisp and crumbled, plus more for garnish if desired, 2 cherry tomatoes, seeded and finely chopped, 1 Tbs. dried parsley flakes, salt and pepper to taste. Garnish with additional bacon pieces.

Classic: 1 tsp. prepared mustard*, 1 Tbs. diced dill pickle*, 1 tsp. honey, dust with paprika.

Oven Baked Tortilla

Makes 48 bite-sized squares

In Spain, a "tortilla" is an oven-cooked omelet and can be eaten with the fingers at room temperature. Perfect for a small serving or appetizer, these tasty squares, adapted from "Easy Tapas" by Parragon Press, are fun, full of good things, and easy to make.

4 Tbs. olive oil
1 large garlic clove, minced
4 green onions, white and green parts finely chopped
1 green bell pepper, seeded and finely diced
1 red bell pepper, seeded and finely diced
1½ c. cauliflower, boiled until tender and diced
5 large eggs
scant ½ c. homemade yogurt*
6 oz. Cheddar or Parmesan cheese*, freshly grated (about 1½ c.)
salt and pepper

Preheat oven to 375°. Line a 7 x 10 inch baking dish with foil or parchment and brush with a little olive oil. Set aside.

Place the olive oil, garlic, green onions, and bell peppers in a non-stick skillet and cook over medium heat, stirring, for 10 minutes. Let cool, then stir in the cooked cauliflower. Cool.

Beat the eggs, yogurt, and cheese together in a large bowl. Stir the cooled vegetables into the bowl and season to taste with salt and pepper.

Pour the mixture into the baking dish and smooth the top. Bake for 30-40 minutes, or until golden brown, puffed, and set in the center. Remove from oven and let cool and set. Run a spatula around the edge, then invert onto a sheet pan, browned side up, and peel off the foil or parchment. If the surface looks a little runny, place under a medium broiler to dry out.

Cool completely. Trim edges if necessary, then cut into 48 squares. Serve on a platter with wooden toothpicks.

*See page 7 for an explanation of what makes this ingredient legal for the Specific Carbohydrate Diet.

Food With Friends

Spinach Mushroom Tortilla

Serves 6-8 for tapas

Our classy and pretty oven-cooked omelet, or "tortilla," is a perfectly tasty, nourishing tapas dish!

Note: To toast almonds, stir constantly in a dry skillet over medium heat until fragrant and beginning to brown. Pour onto a plate to stop cooking.

2 Tbs. olive oil
3 shallots, finely chopped
12 oz. mushrooms, sliced
10 oz. fresh, washed baby spinach
2 oz. (generous 1/3 c.) toasted slivered almonds
5 eggs
2 Tbs. fresh parsley, chopped
2 Tbs. homemade yogurt*
3 oz. (generous ¾ c.) freshly grated Parmesan cheese*

Preheat oven to 375°. Line a 7x10 inch baking dish with foil or parchment and brush with a little olive oil. Set aside.

Sauté shallots in olive oil over low heat, stirring occasionally, for 3-5 minutes. Add mushrooms; cook, stirring frequently, for 4 minutes. Increase heat to medium; add spinach in a few batches, stirring to help it wilt, and cook 3-4 minutes, stirring frequently. Reduce heat; season with salt and pepper to taste. Stir in almonds. Cool.

See page 7 for an explanation of what makes this ingredient legal for the Specific Carbohydrate Diet.

Beat eggs with parsley and yogurt in a bowl. Stir in the cooled vegetables; season to taste with salt and pepper.

Pour mixture into prepared baking dish; smooth top. Bake for 30-40 minutes; sprinkle with parmesan cheese during last 10 minutes. Bake until golden, puffed, and set in the center. Remove from the oven; allow to cool and set. Run a knife around the edge; invert onto a sheet pan; peel off foil or parchment. If the surface looks runny, place under a medium broiler to dry out.

Cool completely. Trim the edges if necessary; cut into long thin wedges. For a different presentation, the tortilla may also be cut into 48 squares and served on a platter with wooden toothpicks. Serve lukewarm or cold.

Chicken Salad with Raisins & Nuts

Serves 6-8 for Tapas

A delicious meat salad to serve with whole green or black olives and some of our other tapas recipes, for a grand spread. Our tasters gave this one a 10!

- **2 Tbs. red wine vinegar***
- **2 Tbs. honey**
- **1 bay leaf**
- **Pared rind of half of 1 lemon**
- **½ c. raisins**
- **2 large boneless chicken breasts, partially frozen**
- **3 Tbs. olive oil**
- **1 garlic clove, finely chopped**
- **½ c. slivered almonds**
- **3 Tbs. olive oil**
- **1 small bunch fresh cilantro or flat-leaf parsley, finely chopped**
- **salt and pepper to taste**

To make dressing, combine vinegar, honey, bay leaf, and lemon rind in a pan and bring to a boil. Remove from heat; stir in raisins and set aside to cool.

Slice partially frozen chicken widthwise into very thin slices. Heat oil in a large skillet; add chicken and cook over medium heat, stirring occasionally, for 8-10 minutes, or until lightly browned. Add garlic and nuts and cook, stirring constantly and shaking the skillet, for 1 minute, until nuts are golden. Season to taste with salt and pepper.

Pour cooled dressing into a large bowl, discarding the bay leaf and lemon rind. Add 3 Tbs. oil and whisk together. Season to taste with salt and pepper; add chicken mixture and cilantro or parsley and toss. Turn the salad into a serving dish and serve warm, or if serving cold, cover and chill in refrigerator for 2-3 hours before serving.

Background credit: FreePik

Food With Friends

Tasty Chicken Wings

Makes 12 tapas servings

These flavorful chicken wings are a variation on buffalo wings, and are served with celery and dip. They're a fun tapas main dish. We served these wings at our NoMoreCrohns pirate party and the little pirates loved them! The recipe is adapted from Sunset, and includes 4 baking sauces and 2 dips. See website for our games!

4 pounds chicken wings
Baking sauces (right)
2 bunches celery
Salt
Dipping Sauces (right)

Rinse chicken wings and pat dry. Cut apart at joints with meat scissors, snipping away thicker pieces of skin while you're at it. Reserve little wing tips for making chicken broth, if desired.

Line each of two baking sheets with a single piece of 12-inch wide heavy foil, pinching a ridge of foil about ¾ inch high across the middle of each pan if you want to flavor the wings with 4 different baking sauces (omit ridge if using only 1 or 2 sauces). Grease the foil with oil. Arrange about 1 pound of wings in each half of each pan.

Bake wings, uncovered, in a 400° oven until golden brown, 30 to 35 minutes. Remove pans from oven and pour baking sauce of your choice over each 1-pound portion of wings, turning wings to coat well. Return wings to oven and bake until sauce is bubbling and edges of wings are crisp, about 15 more minutes; turn wings once or twice.

*See page 7 for an explanation of what makes this ingredient legal for the Specific Carbohydrate Diet.

Meanwhile, break celery stalks from bunch, rinse well and cut in half. Arrange hot or room-temperature wings and celery in a basket or on a tray. Salt chicken and celery to taste. Spoon 1 or 2 dipping sauces into small bowls. Serve wings and celery to swish through dipping sauces.

Baking Sauces for Tasty Chicken Wings

Choose from the following; each is enough to season 1 pound of wings. You can double, triple or quadruple each recipe. If made ahead, cover and refrigerate for up to 1 week.

Red Hot Sauce. Stir together 2 Tbs. *each* apple cider vinegar* and water, 1 Tbs. tomato juice*, 1 tsp. honey, 1 to 3 tsp. hot pepper sauce* (less for mild heat), and ¼ to 1 tsp. cayenne (less for mild heat).

Ginger Sauce. In a food processor or blender, whirl 2 Tbs. chopped fresh ginger, 2 Tbs. *each* honey and pineapple juice* and 1 Tbs. apple cider vinegar* until smoothly pureed.

Garlic Sauce. In a 6- to 8-inch frying pan, combine ¼ c. minced or pressed garlic and 1 Tbs. olive oil; stir over medium heat until garlic is light gold. Pour into a blender or food processor and add 2 Tbs. pineapple juice*; 2 tsp. *each* lemon juice, apple cider vinegar*, and minced fresh or dry rosemary; and ½ tsp. drained capers. Whirl until smoothly pureed.

Mustard Sauce. Mix 2 Tbs. *each* honey and prepared mustard*, 1 Tbs. apple cider vinegar*, and 1 tsp. pepper.

Dipping Sauces for Tasty Chicken Wings

Ranch Yogurt Dip. Stir together 2 c. homemade yogurt*, ½ c. homemade mayonnaise*, p. 176, ¼ c. minced green onions (including tops), 2 Tbs. dried parsley, crushed, ½ tsp. minced or crushed garlic, ½ to 1 tsp. salt, or to taste.

Blue Cheese* Dip. Fold several layers of heavy paper towels and spread with 3 c. homemade yogurt*. Top with several more layers of paper towel. Allow to sit for 5 to 10 minutes, turning once, then remove top toweling and scrape thickened yogurt into a bowl with a rubber spatula. Coarsely mash ¼ pound blue veined cheese* with a fork and stir into yogurt cheese. Add 1 tsp. minced garlic, ½ tsp. dry mustard, and 1/8 tsp. pepper.

Note: A full recipe of either of these sauces is enough to accompany 4 pounds of chicken wings. If you want to serve both, divide each recipe in half. If made ahead, cover and refrigerate for up to 3 days.

Asian Lettuce Wraps

Serves 6-8 for tapas

While Asian food isn't what you would find in a tapas bar in Spain, it fits perfectly in this section because it can be served on a platter for everyone and small servings can be wrapped in lettuce and eaten with your fingers. This is a delicious and fun dish, inspired by similar appetizer plates at The Rainforest Cafe and Chili's. The peanut-tomato sauce is a great accompaniment to the flavorful chicken and crunchy veggies.

Note: Freezing the chicken for 20 minutes will make it easier to slice into thin pieces.

1 head butter lettuce or iceberg lettuce, rinsed and separated
4 boneless, skinless chicken breasts
4-5 large carrots, grated
1 large onion, peeled, stem and root removed
1 head broccoli, chopped
½ c. sliced almonds
2 Tbs. sesame seeds*
toasted sesame oil for frying

Peanut Sauce:
toasted sesame oil for frying
1/3 tsp. crushed garlic
½ c. peanut butter*
1½ c. tomato juice*
1 Tbs. honey
¼ tsp. hot pepper sauce*

To make sauce, sauté crushed garlic in 1 Tbs. sesame oil for 1 minute, or until fragrant. Add remaining ingredients. Heat on low, stirring occasionally.

Slice chicken crosswise into thin, bite-size strips. Cut onion into thin wedges, making long thin pieces.

Stir-fry onion and chicken in 1 Tbs. sesame oil for about 4 minutes until meat is no longer pink and onion begins to brown, in batches if necessary. Remove to a plate. In the same pan, stir-fry broccoli, sesame seeds, and sliced almonds in 1 Tbs. sesame oil until broccoli is bright green, and almonds are slightly browned, 2-3 minutes.

To serve, on a platter place separate piles of lettuce, chicken mixture, broccoli mixture, and grated carrots, along with tongs or serving spoons. Serve with warm peanut sauce. To eat, place some of each item in a lettuce leaf, top with sauce and eat with your fingers.

Chicken In Lemon & Garlic

Serves 6-8 for Tapas

Serve this delicious lemony chicken with a stack of small plates so everyone at the table can take what they want.

- **4 large boneless chicken breasts**
- **3 Tbs. olive oil**
- **1 onion, finely chopped**
- **6 large garlic cloves, minced**
- **2 lemons; 1 with rind pared and thinly sliced, 1 with rind zested, both juiced**
- **4 Tbs. parsley, chopped**
- **Salt and pepper**
- **Lemon wedges, to serve**

Note: Freezing the chicken for 20 minutes will make it easier to slice into thin pieces.

Slice chicken widthwise into very thin slices. Set aside.

Heat olive oil in a large skillet, add onion and cook on medium heat for 5 minutes, until softened and lightly browned. Add garlic and cook an additional 30 seconds.

Add chicken to skillet, separating meat, and cook gently for 5-10 minutes, stirring from time to time, until all ingredients are lightly browned and chicken is tender.

Add lemon zest and lemon juice, increase heat, and let it bubble. At the same time, deglaze the skillet by scraping and stirring all sediment on the bottom of the skillet into the juices with a wooden spoon. Remove skillet from heat, stir in the parsley, and season to taste with plenty of salt and pepper.

Transfer chicken mixture, piping hot, to a warmed serving dish. Sprinkle with pared lemon peel, and serve with lemon wedges for squeezing over chicken.

Chicken & Olive Roll-Ups

Serves 6-8 for Tapas

These very tasty and pretty chicken slices make a great snack or are perfect as part of a "small plate" tapas meal. Adapted slightly from "Easy Tapas."

> **2/3 c. chopped black olives***
> **1/3 c. butter*, softened**
> **4 Tbs. fresh parsley, finely chopped**
> **4 boneless chicken breasts**
> **2 Tbs. olive oil**

Preheat oven to 400°. Combine olives, butter, and parsley together in a bowl; set aside.

Slice chicken breasts horizontally most of the way through, then open like a book, creating a thin layer of chicken, pounding a few times if needed to even the thickness. Spread olive mixture over chicken breasts; roll up and secure with wooden toothpicks or tie with cooking string. (May freeze at this point for later.)

Thaw chicken rolls if frozen. Place chicken rolls in a large baking dish. Drizzle oil over them and bake for 45-50 minutes, or until tender and the juices run clear when the chicken is pierced with the point of a sharp knife.

Transfer rolls to a cutting board and discard toothpicks or string. Using a very sharp knife, cut into slices, then transfer to warmed serving plates and serve.

Porterhouse Steak with Garlic

Serves 6-8 for tapas

4 porterhouse steaks, about 6-8 oz. each and 1-inch thick
5 garlic cloves
salt and pepper
3 Tbs. olive oil
1/3 c. dry white wine or apple cider*
chopped flat-leaf parsley for garnish

Cut steaks into 1-inch cubes and put in a large, shallow dish. Slice 3 of the garlic cloves and set aside. Finely chop the remaining 2 garlic cloves and sprinkle over the steak cubes. Season generously with pepper and mix together well. Cover and let marinate in the refrigerator for 1-2 hours. These may be done ahead and frozen.

Heat oil in a large skillet; add reserved garlic slices and cook over low heat, stirring, for 1 minute, or until golden. Increase heat to medium-high; add thawed (if frozen) steak cube mixture and cook, stirring constantly, for 2-3 minutes, until browned and almost cooked to your liking.

Add wine or cider, and cook until it has evaporated slightly. Season to taste with salt and turn into a warmed serving dish. Garnish with chopped parsley and serve hot.

See page 7 for an explanation of what makes this ingredient legal for the Specific Carbohydrate Diet.

Paprika Spareribs

Serves 6 for Tapas

- Olive oil, for oiling pan
- 2 pounds pork spareribs, have butcher cut in half
- 1/3 c. dry white wine
- 5 tsp. smoked paprika
- 2 garlic cloves, minced
- 1 Tbs. dried oregano, crushed
- 2/3 c. water
- salt

Preheat oven to 425°. Oil a large roasting pan. Cut sheet of spareribs into individual ribs. Put spareribs in the roasting pan in a single layer; roast for 20 minutes. Meanwhile, make the sauce by combining wine, paprika, garlic, oregano, water, and salt to taste in a pitcher.

Reduce oven to 350°. Pour off fat from ribs; pour sauce over spareribs and turn ribs to coat on both sides. Roast for an additional 45 minutes, basting ribs with sauce once halfway through or adding water to pan, if needed, until ribs are tender. Pile ribs onto a serving dish; serve hot.

Mini Pork Brochettes

Makes 12

Marinating over night creates great flavor!

- 1 pound lean boneless pork
- 1 Tbs. olive oil
- 1 tsp. grated rind and juice of 1 large lemon
- 2 cloves garlic, crushed
- 2 Tbs. chopped fresh flat-leaf parsley, plus extra to garnish
- 1 Tbs. Moroccan spice mix, p. 177
- salt and pepper

Cut pork into 36 bite size cubes; place in a large zip-top plastic bag. To prepare marinade, combine all remaining ingredients. Reserve 4 Tbs. of marinade. Pour remaining marinade over pork in bag and squish it around. Refrigerate for 8 hours or overnight, squishing bag of pork two or three times.

Preheat broiler, grill pan or grill to medium-high heat. Thread 3 pork pieces, leaving space between each piece, onto each skewer. Cook the brochettes for 10-15 minutes, until tender and lightly charred, turning and basting with reserved marinade. Serve brochettes hot, garnished with parsley.

Background credit: FreePik

Spanish Meatballs

Serves 6-8 for Tapas

Smoked paprika gives these meatballs deep flavor and low, slow, cooking ensures they're extra tender. Adapted from MarthaStewart.com, the meatballs will also taste great made with ground turkey* or beef or a combination. When I go to our local tapas restaurant, I always order the meatballs - they're delicious!

1 pound ground pork*
½ medium onion, finely chopped
¾ tsp. ground cumin
2 tsp. smoked paprika
3 Tbs. almond flour
1 large egg, lightly beaten
2 Tbs. chopped fresh parsley
1 tsp. salt
¼ tsp. ground pepper
2 Tbs. extra-virgin olive oil

Sauce:
1/3 c. tomato juice*
2 Tbs. finely chopped onion
½ tsp. smoked paprika
2 c. diced fresh tomatoes

In a large bowl, combine pork, onion, cumin, paprika, almond flour, egg, and parsley. Season with salt and pepper. With a wooden spoon, gently mix to combine and, using your hands, roll into 12 meatballs.

In a large nonstick skillet, heat 1 tablespoons oil over medium-high. In two batches, brown meatballs on all sides. Gently transfer meatballs to a 5- to 6-quart crock pot.

Add onions for sauce to skillet; cook until fragrant. Add tomato juice, paprika, and diced tomatoes. Stir to deglaze pan. Pour over meatballs in crock pot. Season with additional salt and pepper. Cook on LOW until meatballs are tender, 5 hours.

*See page 7 for an explanation of what makes this ingredient legal for the Specific Carbohydrate Diet.

Food With Friends

Falafel with Cucumber Salad

Makes about 16 patties

Falafel is a delicious Middle Eastern patty or ball that is usually made from garbanzo beans and seasonings. When served as a main dish, falafel is served with bread, such as socca, p. 44, or pita for non-SCDers, along with lettuce, tomatoes, and tahini. This recipe, adapted from Saveur Magazine, uses navy beans you've soaked overnight and partially cooked; the beans will finish cooking as you bake the falafel. They're delicious with our tzatziki sauce and cucumber salad, following, and we also like to add orange slices and date slivers when we eat them.

For Falafel:
½ pound dried navy beans, soaked overnight in plenty of water and drained
1 c. roughly chopped flat-leaf parsley
2 tsp. coconut flour
¾ tsp. ground coriander
¾ tsp. ground cumin
3 cloves garlic, smashed
1 small onion, roughly chopped
cayenne pepper, to taste
2 eggs, lightly beaten
1½ tsp. baking soda mixed with 1 Tbs. water
1½ tsp. salt, or to taste

For Tzatziki Sauce:
1 large cucumber, peeled, seeded, grated
2 c. homemade yogurt*
1 green onion, thinly sliced
1 Tbs. *each;* fresh parsley and fresh mint
½ tsp. *each;* salt, ground cumin, and honey

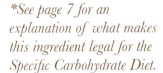

*See page 7 for an explanation of what makes this ingredient legal for the Specific Carbohydrate Diet.

For Cucumber Salad:
3 tomatoes, chopped
2 cucumbers, peeled, seeded, and chopped
½ small red onion, finely chopped and soaked in water for 15 minutes to mellow flavor (or may be briefly cooked)
3 Tbs. lemon juice
½ c. flat-leaf parsley, chopped, packed
2 Tbs. olive oil
½ tsp. salt

For falafel, drain beans after soaking, then place in a saucepan and cover with plenty of fresh water. Boil hard for 25 minutes; drain and cool. Place partially cooked beans in a food processor with parsley, coconut flour, coriander, cumin, garlic, onions, and cayenne.

Pulse mixture until it is well combined yet still coarse in texture, about 40 pulses, scraping down as needed. Add eggs and baking soda mixture, and season with salt; pulse to combine. Chill mixture in the freezer for 20 minutes.

Preheat oven to 400°. Place parchment on 2 baking sheets. (Parchment keeps patties from sticking and breaking apart.) Make about 16 patties of falafel mixture on the baking sheets, leaving space for them to spread; bake for 20 minutes. Remove from oven and flip patties with a spatula. At this point you can brush patties with oil for a crispier crust; patties in photo were not brushed with oil. Bake for 10 more minutes. Serve with tzatziki sauce.

For sauce: Place grated cucumber between two stacks of paper towels for 5 minutes, absorbing as much moisture as possible. Combine with yogurt, green onion, herbs, salt, cumin, and honey. Adjust seasonings.

For salad: In a large bowl, toss together tomatoes, cucumbers, red onion, lemon juice, parsley, olive oil, and salt. Serve falafel with salad and tzatziki sauce. Fold inside thin slices of warmed flatbread, if desired.

Delicious socca bread plus pita for the non-SCDers, separated to avoid contamination.

Tapas Side Dishes

Asparagus, Bacon & Almonds, 118

Seasoned Almonds, 118

Fattoush Country Salad, 119

Avocado Citrus Salad, 119

Figs with Blue Cheese, 120

Mexican Skillet Cakes, 121

Zucchini Tabbouleh, 122

Lima Beans & Bacon, 122

Marinated Artichoke Hearts, 123

Garlic Mushrooms, 123

Background credit: FreePik

Roasted Asparagus, with Bacon & Almonds

Serves 4-6 for tapas

3 slices pre-cooked bacon, cut into 1-inch pieces
12 asparagus spears, woody ends broken off
¼ c. whole almonds
1 Tbs. olive oil
salt

Preheat oven to 400°. Place asparagus spears, bacon pieces, and almonds on a baking sheet. Drizzle with oil; stir around to coat everything with oil. Sprinkle with salt.

Roast 9 to 10 minutes, stirring once. Serve hot.

Seasoned Almonds

Serves 6-8 for tapas

1 Tbs. olive oil
2/3 c. whole blanched or unblanched almonds
kosher salt
1 tsp. paprika or ground cumin

Preheat oven to 350°. Place olive oil on a cookie sheet and swirl it around so it covers the pan. Add almonds and toss on the pan so they are evenly coated in oil, then shake them into a single layer.

Roast almonds for 20 minutes, or until light brown, stirring several times during cooking. Drain almonds on paper towels, then transfer to a bowl.

While almonds are still warm, sprinkle with plenty of salt and spice, and toss together to coat. Serve warm or cold. The almonds are at their best when served freshly cooked, however they can be stored in an airtight container for up to 3 days.

Fattoush Country Salad

Serves 6-8 for tapas

This simple and flavor-packed peasant salad is a popular dish all over the Middle East. Feel free to add more parsley, mint, or cilantro to taste.

1 yellow or red bell pepper, roughly chopped
1 large cucumber, peeled and chopped
4-5 tomatoes, chopped
1 bunch green onions (7 or 8 onions), chopped
2 Tbs. *each;* chopped fresh parsley, mint, & cilantro

2 cloves garlic, crushed
5 Tbs. olive oil
juice of 2 lemons
salt and pepper

Combine bell pepper, cucumber, and tomatoes in a large salad bowl and mix together. Stir in the green onions. Add the parsley, mint, and cilantro.

To make the dressing, shake together the garlic, olive oil, and lemon juice in a jar with a tight fitting lid, then season to taste with salt and pepper. Pour the dressing over the salad and toss lightly to mix.

Avocado Citrus Salad

Serves 6-8 for tapas

2 pink grapefruit
2 large navel oranges
2 c. baby arugula or chopped lettuce
2 avocados, sliced
2 radishes, trimmed and thinly sliced
2 Tbs. olive oil
2 green onions, thinly sliced
Coarse salt and ground pepper

Remove peel and pith of grapefruit and oranges (how-to on p. 177). Working over a bowl, cut out grapefruit and orange segments, saving juice. Place arugula or lettuce on a platter and top with avocados, radishes, and citrus segments with juices. Drizzle with oil, top with green onions, and season with salt and pepper.

Note: If you don't have ripe avocados, you can substitute 2 Persian cucumbers, sliced.

Figs with Blue Cheese

Serve 6-8 for Tapas

Substitute wedges of pear if you are unable to find fresh figs. Halve the drizzled honey if using pears. Our tasters loved this dish, even if Blue cheese wasn't their favorite cheese! It's just so good!

12 ripe figs
1 c. Spanish Blue cheese*, crumbled
¾ c. whole almonds
2 Tbs. honey
honey for drizzling

Stir together almonds and honey in a non-stick sauté pan. Stir over medium heat until bubbling. Allow nuts and honey to cook in an even layer, stirring occasionally, about 3 minutes. Pour onto a plate to cool. Set aside; break apart.

To serve, cut figs in halves or quarters and arrange 4-5 pieces on individual small plates, or arrange all pieces on a platter. Coarsely chop almonds by hand. Place a mound of blue cheese in the center of the fruit and sprinkle fruit with chopped almonds. Lightly drizzle honey on fruit.

Photo credit: Pexels

*See page 7 for an explanation of what makes this ingredient legal for the Specific Carbohydrate Diet.

Mexican Skillet Cakes

Makes about 12 cakes

Mexican flavored veggies packed into a flapjack, and topped with creamy guacamole! A perfect way to serve a tapas portion of veggies.

1 red onion, diced (reserve 1 Tbs. for guacamole)
2 tsp. cumin
3 tsp. paprika
½ tsp. *each;* **dried oregano leaves and black pepper**
¼ tsp. hot pepper sauce*

1 red bell pepper, diced
1 zucchini, diced
4 mushrooms, diced

2 eggs, beaten with a fork
1 cup almond flour
½ tsp. baking soda (add to almond flour)
½ tsp. salt

Guacamole

Combine and mash with a fork:

1 avocado, peeled
squeeze of lime
1 garlic clove, grated or minced
1 Tbs. red onion (reserved, left)
cilantro, for garnish
salt to taste

Sauté onion in 2 tsp. **olive oil** with the cumin, paprika, oregano, pepper, and hot pepper sauce, for about 3 minutes, adding a little water, as needed.

Meanwhile, combine bell pepper, zucchini, and mushrooms in a large bowl. After the onions have softened, add them to the bowl and toss to combine everything. Stir in the eggs, almond flour, baking soda, and salt.

Rub a clean skillet with olive oil. Heat it to medium high. Place ¼ cup portions of batter into the skillet and flatten slightly. Let them cook for about 4 minutes per side, until brown. Carefully flip once with a spatula, helping with a silicone scraper. Repeat until all batter is cooked, adding more oil with each batch.

While they're cooking, make your guacamole by combining everything in a bowl and mashing it with the back of a fork.

To assemble, top your skillet cakes with a dollop of guacamole, a sprig of cilantro, and a squeeze of lime.

Zucchini Tabbouleh

Serves 6-8 for tapas

Chopped zucchini replaces bulgar in this flavorful salad adapted from "Eat Well Feel Well." It is an excellent fresh salad to serve in spoonfuls with tapas, or pair with meatball, pp. 73 & 80, olives, fruit, and toasted whole almonds for a meal.

5 medium zucchini, peeled and sliced
1 large bunch fresh parsley, rinsed and stems cut off
1 large bunch fresh mint, rinsed and stems cut off
3 large tomatoes, seeded and finely chopped
7 green onions, white and green parts, thinly sliced

1 tsp. lemon zest
¼ c. olive oil
1 medium shallot, chopped
1 tsp. *each;* minced garlic and salt
¼ tsp. pepper

In a food processor, pulse the zucchini about 20 to 25 times until pieces are small, like couscous. Transfer to a large strainer, mix in a sprinkle of about ½ tsp. salt, and drain for at least 30 minutes. Salt helps pull out the moisture. Press out remaining moisture and place in a large bowl. Chop the parsley and mint leaves in the food processor and add to the zucchini. Stir in the tomatoes and green onions.

In the same food processor, combine the lemon zest, oil, shallot, garlic, salt, and pepper. Pour over salad, mix well, and chill at least 30 minutes.

Lima Beans with Bacon

Serves 4-6 for tapas

2 slices thick bacon, chopped
½ red onion, very finely chopped
1 c. frozen lima beans, boiled 6 minutes and drained
parsley, finely chopped, to taste
salt and pepper to taste
1 Tbs. olive oil

Cook bacon until mostly cooked. Add onion and cook 5 more minutes, until softened. Add cooled beans. Stir in parsley and check seasonings, adding salt and pepper only after tasting. Transfer to a serving bowl and drizzle with oil.

Marinated Artichoke Hearts

1 12-oz. box frozen artichoke hearts, thawed
2/3 c. extra-virgin olive oil
1½ tsp. kosher salt
½ tsp. dried thyme
¾ tsp. dried oregano
1/3 tsp. crushed red chile flakes
4 Tbs. fresh lemon juice

Rinse artichoke hearts under cold water. Combine artichokes, oil, salt, thyme, oregano, and chile flakes in a saucepan set over medium-low heat. Cover and cook, stirring occasionally, until the flavors meld, 10 minutes.

Let cool and stir in lemon juice. Serve or refrigerate in a covered container for up to 1 week.

Garlic Mushrooms

Serves 6-8 for tapas

1 pound white mushrooms
5 Tbs. olive oil
2 garlic cloves, finely chopped
squeeze of lemon juice
4 Tbs. flat-leaf parsley, chopped, plus more for garnish
salt and pepper

Wash and dry mushrooms. Trim off stalks close to the caps, cutting any very large mushrooms in half.

Heat oil in a large skillet; add garlic and cook for 30 seconds, to 1 minute, or until lightly browned. Add mushrooms and sauté over high heat, stirring, until mushrooms have absorbed all the oil, 1 to 2 minutes.

Reduce heat to low. When juices have come out of mushrooms, increase heat again; sauté 4 to 5 minutes, stirring, until juices have almost evaporated. Add lemon juice and season to taste with salt and pepper. Stir in parsley and cook for 1 minute. Transfer mushrooms to warmed serving dish and serve piping hot or warm, garnished with parsley sprigs.

Background credit: FreePik

Food With Friends

Background credit: FreePik

Desserts

Nut Mosaic Tart, 128

Fresh Orange Yogurt Tart, 129

Almond Torte with Grilled Fruit, 130

Yogurt Apple Pie, 131

Butternut Pecan Pie, 132

Erin's Favorite Pumpkin Pie, 133

Yogurt Berry Pie, 134

Lemon Ice-Box Pie, 135

Raspberry Mousse Pie, 136

Angel Pecan Pie, 188

Banana Cream Pie, 189

Hummingbird Cake, 137

Lemon Drizzle Cake, 138

Cocoa Butter Cakes, 139

Dessert Contents, Page 2

Western Fruitcake, 140

Mini Almond Grape Cakes, 141

Valentine Carrot Cakes, 186

Peanut Butter Cake, 187

Banana Ice Cream, 142

Coconut Vanilla Ice Cream, 143

Pumpkin Ice Cream, 143

Vanilla Ice Cream, 144

Cantaloupe Frozen Yogurt, 145

Strawberry Orange Ice in Orange Halves, 146

Crushed Cherry Frozen Yogurt, 147

Frosty Strawberries, 148

Frozen Banana Raspberry Dessert, 191

Watermelon Jello Dessert, 159

Apple Pie Treat, 150

Dessert Contents, Page 3

Real Deal Coconut Macaroons, 151

Coconut Almond Biscotti, 184

Cookie Press Cookies, 152

Peanut Butter Cookies, 153

Peanut Butter Cookie Bars, 154

Lemon Cookies, 185

Cinnamon Cookies, 185

Pork Rind Krispy Treats, 155

Baked Raspberry Custard, 156

Panna Cotta with Raspberries, 157

Bread Pudding, 158

Macaroon Squares with Toppings, 190

English Toffee Candy, 159

Nut Butter Fudge 160

Sugar Plums, 161

Food With Friends

Nut Mosaic Tart

Serves 10 to 12

Make this rich, showy tart, adapted from Sunset Magazine, for your next special event. It's like a pecan pie but with a delicious variety of mixed nuts.

Cheddar Cheese Pie Crust

1½ c. almond flour, somewhat packed
½ c. finely grated sharp Cheddar cheese*
pinch salt
1/3 c. coconut oil, melted
1 Tbs. melted butter*
1-2 Tbs. ice water

Combine almond flour, cheese, and salt. Stir in coconut oil and melted butter. Sprinkle on ice water, stirring. Mixture will stick together. Form into a disk, wrap and freeze 20 minutes or chill one hour. Roll between 2 sheets of plastic wrap. Use as directed. If baking first, bake at 350° 22-25 minutes until brown and firm.

*See page 7 for an explanation of what makes this ingredient legal for the Specific Carbohydrate Diet.

3 cups whole or half unsalted nuts (almonds, walnuts, hazelnuts, macadamias, pistachios, or pecans; use all one kind or equal parts of 3 varieties)
1 Cheddar Cheese Pie Crust, unbaked (recipe left)
3 eggs
1 c. honey
½ tsp. orange zest
1 tsp. vanilla*
¼ c. butter*, melted and cooled slightly
honey-sweetened homemade yogurt* (optional)

Place nuts (if unroasted) in a shallow pan and put in a 350° oven until lightly toasted and beginning to be fragrant, about 10 minutes; cool.

Press Cheddar Cheese Pie Crust evenly over bottom and sides of an 11-inch tart pan with removable bottom.

In a bowl, combine eggs, honey, orange zest, vanilla, and melted butter; beat well until blended. Stir in toasted nuts. Pour into pastry-lined tart pan.

Bake on the bottom rack of a 350° oven until top is golden brown all over, about 33-35 minutes. Let cool on a wire rack. Remove pan sides. Offer wedges with honey-sweetened yogurt.

Fresh Orange & Yogurt Tart

Serves 10

Try this beautiful tart, adapted from Everyday Food, with a topping of other fresh fruits such as pitted and halved cherries, halved grapes, dates cut into matchsticks, kiwi slices, fresh peach slices, halved strawberries, or cooked and cooled apple slices.

- **1 recipe Almond Pie Crust, right**
- **2 tsp. unflavored gelatin**
- **2 ¾ c. homemade yogurt*, divided**
- **½ c. honey**
- **3 tsp. vanilla***
- **½ tsp. salt**
- **3 medium navel oranges**

Almond Pie Crust

1 c. sliced almonds
2/3 c. almond flour
¼ c. honey
¼ c. coconut flour, stirred
½ tsp. salt
6 Tbs. butter*

For the crust; In a food processor, combine sliced almonds, almond flour, honey, coconut flour, and salt. Add butter and pulse until dough holds together and butter is incorporated, scraping down sides as needed with a spatula. Use as directed.

Measure ½ c. of yogurt for filling and set aside. Line a large strainer with coffee filters and pour remaining 2¼ c. yogurt into strainer. Place strainer over a pan or over the sink and allow yogurt to drip while you make the crust or a little longer if you have time. Press dough in bottom and up sides of an 8- to 9-inch cake or pie pan.

Preheat oven to 350°. Place pan on a rimmed baking sheet and bake until crust is golden brown and set, about 20 minutes. Let cool completely on a wire rack.

In a small bowl, sprinkle gelatin over 2 tablespoons **cold water** and let stand 5 minutes. In a small saucepan, warm ½ cup reserved yogurt over medium heat. When it begins to steam, add gelatin mixture and stir until dissolved, about 1 minute.

In a medium bowl, whisk together dripped yogurt, honey, vanilla, and salt. Stir warm gelatin mixture into yogurt mixture. Pour filling into cooled tart shell and refrigerate 2 hours or up to 1 day.

With a sharp paring knife, slice off ends of oranges. Following curve of fruit, cut away peel, removing white pith. Slice oranges into ¼-inch-thick rounds and remove any seeds. Just before serving, arrange orange slices on top of tart.

Almond Torte with Grilled Fruit

Serves 10 to 12

This lightly sweetened torte, adapted from Sunset Magazine, makes a lovely dessert, late-afternoon treat, or even breakfast cake. Almond extract and sliced almonds heighten the flavor and it's delicious topped with juicy grilled fruit.

> ½ c. plus 2 Tbs. unsalted butter*, plus more for pan
> 3 lightly packed cups almond flour
> 1 Tbs. coconut flour
> 1 large egg plus 1 large egg yolk
> 2/3 c. light honey, such as orange blossom
> 2 tsp. *each;* almond extract*, and lemon zest
> 1 tsp. vanilla*
> generous pinch of sea salt (if using unsalted butter)
> 1/3 c. sliced almonds
> 16 ripe figs (or 1 pineapple, sliced, or 8 peach halves)
> 1 c. homemade yogurt*, lightly sweetened with honey

*See page 7 for an explanation of what makes this ingredient legal for the Specific Carbohydrate Diet.

Melt butter and set aside to cool for a few minutes. Put almond flour, coconut flour, egg and yolk, honey, the almond and vanilla extracts, lemon zest, salt, and melted butter in a medium bowl and stir together with a wooden spoon. The batter will be thick and sticky.

Thoroughly butter a 10-inch tart pan with a removable rim. Scoop batter into pan and spread evenly. Chill filled pan in freezer, making sure pan is level, for 20 minutes. Meanwhile, preheat oven to 300°.

Scatter almond slices over top of batter and slide pan into oven. Bake until entire surface is light golden brown, 45 to 50 minutes. (Don't over bake - the torte should be moist.) Set on a rack and let cool completely before serving, about 2 hours.

While torte cools, preheat a grill or grill pan to medium-high. Grill fruit until juicy and warmed through, 2 to 3 minutes per side. When cool enough to handle, cut into chunks.

Serve slices of torte drizzled with honey, if desired, dolloped with sweetened yogurt and topped with pieces of grilled fruit.

Yogurt Apple Pie

Makes one 9-inch pie

Adapted from Rodale's Naturally Delicious Desserts and Snacks, this apple pie tastes just like it's supposed to… old fashioned, sweet, and fruity. Erin described it as "to die for."

- **1 Cheddar Cheese Pie Crust, p. 128, unbaked**
- **5 medium-size tart apples, pared, cored, and sliced**
- **½ c. warmed honey**
- **½ tsp. cinnamon**
- **dash of nutmeg**
- **¼ tsp. salt**

Topping:
- **1-1/3 c. homemade yogurt***
- **2-3 Tbs. honey**
- **1 tsp. vanilla***

Preheat oven to 425°. Press crust into a pie pan.

Arrange half the apples over the crust. Combine honey, cinnamon, nutmeg, and salt. Drizzle half the mixture over the apples. Repeat layer of apples, then honey mixture. Bake in preheated oven for 10 minutes, then reduce heat to 375° and bake 30 minutes longer, or until apples are tender. Wrap a strip of foil around edges of crust half way through to prevent it from becoming too brown. Remove from the oven and allow to cool.

Meanwhile, pour yogurt onto a thick stack of paper towels, then cover with another stack. Allow to sit for 5 to 10 minutes, flipping once. Scrape into a bowl with a rubber spatula and stir in other topping ingredients.

Top cooled pie with yogurt topping. If desired, garnish top with a pinch of cinnamon and/or chopped nuts. Serve at room temperature or cold.

Background credit: FreePik

Butternut Pecan Pie

Serves 8

Taste tests conducted with eight non-SCD tasters showed that this pie is very good, has a satisfying amount of sweetness and just the right quantity of pecan pie topping. We think you'll enjoy serving it for your Thanksgiving, or any time you want a comforting, tasty dessert. It's great with vanilla ice cream, p. 144.

3½ c. cooked and mashed butternut squash (or pumpkin)
3 eggs, lightly beaten
2 tsp. vanilla*
1 tsp. cinnamon
½ tsp. ginger
¼ tsp. cloves
1/3 to ½ c. honey (to taste)

Topping:
¾ c. pecan halves
1 egg, lightly beaten
1/3 c. honey
1 Tbs. butter*, melted
1 tsp. vanilla*

Butter a pie pan and preheat oven to 350°. Place squash in a mixing bowl. Add 3 eggs, vanilla, cinnamon, ginger, cloves, and honey. Combine thoroughly and pour into prepared pan.

Combine topping ingredients. Gently spoon over filling, evenly distributing pecans. Place pie on a sheet pan and bake for 50 to 60 minutes, or until filling is firm when shaken and a knife inserted near the center comes out clean. Cool. Refrigerate leftovers.

Erin's Favorite Pumpkin Pie

Serves 6

Erin loves the recipe from Against All Grain with our Cheddar Cheese Pie Crust, and makes it all the time with a few minor adaptations.

> 1 recipe Cheddar Cheese Pie Crust, unbaked, p. 128
> 1 15-oz. can pumpkin puree* (or about 2 c. fresh)
> 3 eggs + 1 egg yolk
> ½ c. almond milk*
> ½ c. honey
> ¼ tsp. *each;* salt, ground cloves, ground cardamom
> ½ tsp. *each;* ground nutmeg and lemon zest
> 1 tsp. *each;* vanilla,* ground ginger, and ground cinnamon

Preheat oven to 350°. Line a pie pan with pie crust, crimping the edges. In a large bowl, whisk together the pumpkin, eggs, yolk, almond milk, honey, salt, cloves, cardamom, nutmeg, zest, vanilla, ginger, and cinnamon until completely mixed.

Pour filling into the unbaked pie crust. Bake for 45-55 minutes, or until a knife blade, inserted near the center, comes out clean. If the crust starts to brown too quickly, cover the edges with foil and continue baking.

*See page 7 for an explanation of what makes this ingredient legal for the Specific Carbohydrate Diet.

Artwork credit: RequestReduce.org

Yogurt Berry Pie

Serves 6-8

This pie makes a beautiful Valentine's Day dessert!

Nut Crust

In a food processor, whirl 1¾ c. roasted **pecans** until coarsely chopped. To nuts, add 3 Tbs. **honey** and 4 Tbs. **butter***, cut into chunks. Whirl until mixture holds together. Spread dough evenly over bottom and sides of a 9-inch pie pan. Bake at 350° for 12 to 15 minutes or until beginning to brown. Cool completely.

1 recipe nut crust, cooled (left)
2½ c. homemade yogurt*
1½ c. unsweetened apple cider*
½ c. honey
2 pkg. unflavored gelatin (about 4 tsp.)
½ tsp. vanilla*
6 c. frozen mixed berries, almost thawed
Fresh mint for garnish, if desired

Make yogurt into dripped yogurt cheese (see instructions p. 10). Boil apple cider until reduced to 1¼ cups, about 20 minutes. Soften gelatin in ½ c. **water** for 5 minutes, then stir into hot apple cider, stirring until dissolved. Stir in honey. Cool to room temperature.

In a medium bowl, thoroughly combine **half** of the juice mixture, vanilla, and yogurt cheese. Spread yogurt mixture into cooled crust.

In a large bowl, gently toss cold berries with remaining cooled juice/gelatin mixture until juice is thickened. Spoon gently onto yogurt mixture. Cover; chill for 3 to 6 hours. If desired, garnish with mint and/or serve with Honey Lemon Curd, p. 138

Artwork credit: Pixabay

Lemon Ice-Box Pie
"A Slice of Friendship!"

Serves 6-8

This light and lemony pie, adapted from BHG, can be made ahead and served straight from the fridge.

Cheddar Cheese Pie Crust, p. 128, baked and cooled
1 c. honey
1½ envelopes unflavored gelatin (about 3 tsp.)
1 Tbs. lemon zest
6 Tbs. lemon juice
6 Tbs. water
6 egg yolks, lightly beaten
¼ c. butter*, cut up
4 c. homemade yogurt*
Candied Lemon Slices (optional garnish, right)
Fresh mint leaves (optional garnish)

In a medium saucepan combine honey and gelatin. Add lemon zest, lemon juice, and water. Cook and stir over medium heat until thickened and bubbly.

Whisk half the honey mixture into the egg yolks, whisking constantly to prevent the yolks from cooking. Return egg mixture to saucepan. Cook, stirring constantly, over medium heat until mixture comes to a gentle boil. Cook and stir 2 minutes more. Remove from heat. Add cut-up butter, stirring until melted. Transfer to a bowl; cover with plastic wrap. Cool 20 minutes.

Place yogurt in a large bowl; gradually stir in lemon mixture. Carefully spoon into baked crust-lined pan. Cover and chill overnight. To serve, top pie with Candied Lemon Slices and fresh mint, if desired.

Candied Lemon Slices

1 c. honey
1 c. water
2 lemons, sliced thin

In a large skillet combine honey and water. Cook and stir over medium heat until honey is dissolved. Bring mixture to a boil; reduce heat. Add lemon slices. Cook for 1 minute, turning once. Transfer slices to waxed paper to cool.

*See page 7 for an explanation of what makes this ingredient legal for the Specific Carbohydrate Diet.

Raspberry Mousse Pie

Serves 8

A slice of this pretty pink pie is nice with a dollop of honey-sweetened homemade yogurt* and raspberries.

> 1¼ c. almond flour or almond meal
> 1 egg white
> 3 Tbs. honey
> 2 Tbs. butter, melted
>
> 1½ c. homemade yogurt*
> 1 envelope unflavored gelatin (about 2 tsp.)
> 2½ c. fresh or frozen raspberries + ¼ c. reserved
> ½ c. honey

*See page 7 for an explanation of what makes this ingredient legal for the Specific Carbohydrate Diet.

Preheat oven to 350° (325° if using a glass pan). Butter a 9-inch pie plate. Place almond flour, egg white, honey, and butter in a food processor and process until blended. Use a rubber spatula to press mixture onto the bottom and up the sides of the pie plate. Bake for 8-10 minutes or until set. While still hot, gently run a sharp knife between pan and crust to release sides. Cool completely.

Meanwhile, spread yogurt on a stack of thick paper towels and cover with more paper towels. Allow to rest for 5 to 10 minutes, turning once. Scrape into a bowl with a rubber spatula.

In a small saucepan, sprinkle gelatin over ½ c. **cold water**; let stand for 1 minute. Heat over low heat, stirring until gelatin is completely dissolved. Remove from the heat; set aside. Puree raspberries in food processor; press through a strainer, discarding seeds. Thoroughly combine puree, yogurt, honey, and gelatin mixture in a large bowl; cover and refrigerate for 40 minutes or until partially set.

Remove raspberry mixture from refrigerator and, using a rubber spatula, gently fold in remaining ¼ c. raspberries and spread evenly into cooled crust. Cover and refrigerate for at least 3 hours.

Hummingbird Cake

Serves 8-10

This classic Southern cake is delicious and adapts very well to the SCD. Make sure the center is fully cooked before removing the cake from the oven. The cake pictured is a ½ recipe, baked in a 6-inch springform pan placed on a cookie sheet, then split. (To halve the eggs, use one whole egg and one egg yolk.) Start with the icing, so the yogurt has time to drip and thicken or use the Buttercream Icing on p. 54.

- 3 c. almond or pecan flour
- 2/3 c. honey
- 3 eggs
- ¼ c. melted butter*
- 1 tsp. baking soda
- 2 speckled bananas, mashed
- ¼ c. chopped nuts
- 1 c. fresh pineapple, finely chopped, save and include juices
- 1 tsp. vanilla*
- 1 tsp. salt
- ½ tsp. cinnamon

Mix together all ingredients using a whisk or beater. Transfer batter to a greased ring mold or Bundt pan. Bake at 350° for 45 to 50 minutes or until a toothpick inserted in the center comes out clean and top springs back when lightly touched.

Cool in pan for about 10 minutes; gently run a knife down the sides. Place a serving plate on top of cake, and invert onto the serving plate. Cool completely, then spread with icing (recipe, right) and decorate with pesticide free edible flowers, or chopped nuts if desired. Refrigerate leftovers.

Icing

- 1½ c. homemade yogurt*
- ¼ to 1/3 c. honey or to taste
- ½ tsp. vanilla*
- ½ c. softened butter*
- dash of cinnamon

Place yogurt on a thick stack of paper towels and top with another stack for 5-10 minutes. Scrape into a bowl, and fold in remaining ingredients with a rubber spatula. Drizzle or spread over cooled cake.

Lemon Drizzle Cake

Serves 12-16

When I took this cake to our Easter dinner, it was a big hit with everyone!

Honey Lemon Curd

5 large egg yolks
1 large egg
2/3 c. fresh lemon juice
1 Tbs. finely grated lemon zest
1/3 c. honey (or more to taste)
4 Tbs. unsalted butter*, cut into small pieces

1 c. sifted coconut flour
½ tsp. baking soda
½ c. butter,* soft
½ c. honey
10 eggs
½ c. coconut milk*
1 tsp. lemon juice
1 tsp. salt
zest of 1 lemon

Topping:

Juice of 2 lemons
½ c. honey

In the top of a double boiler or in a heavy pan, whisk together the egg yolks and egg with the lemon juice and honey. Place the double boiler over a pot of simmering water or the heavy pan over very low heat and cook the mixture, whisking constantly, until it becomes pale and thickened, 7 to 10 minutes.

Remove the pan from the heat and immediately pour through a fine strainer to remove any lumps. Whisk the butter in until it has melted. Stir in the lemon zest, cover with wax paper, and let cool to room temperature. Refrigerate in a covered container until chilled, at least 3 hours. Lasts for over a week in the refrigerator.

Preheat oven to 350°. Oil two 8-inch round cake pans. Cover bottoms of pans with rounds of waxed paper or parchment paper. Combine coconut flour and baking soda; set aside.

Beat butter and honey until fluffy. Beat in eggs, coconut milk, lemon juice, salt, and lemon zest. Beat in coconut flour mixture. Divide between pans; Bake 20 to 30 minutes, or until a toothpick inserted in the center comes out clean.

Prick warm cake layers all over with a skewer or meat fork. For topping, thoroughly combine lemon juice and honey; pour over cake. Let cool in the pans, then remove. Spread layers with Honey Lemon Curd (left) or Buttercream Icing, p. 54, blended with lemon zest to taste.

Cocoa Butter Cakes

Makes 6

These mini cakes with a hint of chocolate, sweetened and thickened with dates, are positively decadent! We slightly adapted the recipe which was created by Marilyn, a "Darn Good SCD Cook," and passed on to us by Ruth H., an SCD friend. Top the individual cakes with sweetened yogurt* or buttercream icing, p. 54, and fresh cherries for a scrumptious dessert. Pepper is a secret ingredient that adds just the right "bottom note." Thank you Marilyn, and thank you Ruth!

2 c. lightly stirred pecan or almond flour
½ tsp. salt
¼ tsp. finely ground black pepper
16 large Medjool dates, pitted and chopped (1½ c. chopped dates)
2/3 c. food grade cocoa butter, melted (4 oz.)
2 Tbs. vanilla*
1 egg
½ tsp. baking soda

*See page 7 for an explanation of what makes this ingredient legal for the Specific Carbohydrate Diet.

Place the pecan or almond flour, salt, and pepper in the food processor. Process to mix well. Crumble in the date pieces. Process for 1-2 minutes or until dates and flour are well mixed.

Preheat oven to 325°. Pour melted cocoa butter and vanilla into date mixture. Process again for 1-2 minutes until mixture is pureed.

Add egg and the baking soda and process again until very smooth.

Pour batter into six well-buttered mini-Bundt pans (about the size of a cupcake). Bake for 30-35 minutes or until a toothpick comes out clean and the tops are brown.

Cool cakes and turn out. The cakes taste even more chocolaty if they chill over night before you eat them.

Western Fruitcake

Makes 1 loaf size cake

Bake this beautiful cake ahead of your party and let it cure for up to two months! Loaded with dried fruits and nuts, this cake, adapted from Sunset, is a delicious variation on the traditional cake filled with candied fruit. It slices well when cold, displaying a subtle array of colors from orange-hued apricots, amber dates, to golden raisins. Offer slices of this rich cake for dessert with coffee or tea.

½ c. pitted dates, quartered
1 c. quartered dried apricots
½ c. golden raisins
¾ c. *each;* whole raw almonds and walnut pieces
2 eggs
generous 1/3 c. honey
½ tsp. vanilla*
generous 1/3 c. almond flour, lumps pinched out
¼ tsp. baking soda

Preheat oven to 300°. Generously butter a loaf pan; line the bottom and long sides with parchment, then generously butter paper; set aside.

In a large bowl, thoroughly combine dates, apricots, raisins, almonds, and walnuts. In another bowl, beat eggs with honey and vanilla to blend; add almond flour and baking soda and beat until well blended. With a rubber spatula, fold batter thoroughly into fruit mixture. Spoon into prepared pan and spread evenly, pressing to smooth top.

Bake until a pick comes out dry, or with a few crumbs on it, about 70 to 75 minutes, loosely covering the top with foil part way through if it's getting too brown. Cool in pan on a wire rack for 10 minutes; go down narrow sides with a knife, then turn out of pan. Peel off paper and let cake cool.

Wrap well in foil; chill 2 days or up to 2 months. Slice cold for best results.

Mini Almond Grape Cakes

Makes 9

Inspired by French baking, these small cakes, adapted from Sunset Magazine, are dense with the warm flavors of almond, orange zest, and butter. The grapes become a little jammy after baking, which complements the cakes' richness.

½ c. butter*, at room temperature
2/3 c. honey
2 eggs, at room temperature
1 c. almond flour
4 Tbs. coconut flour (plus more to flour pan)
zest of 1 orange
½ tsp. vanilla*
½ tsp. salt
18 black seedless grapes
1½ Tbs. sliced almonds
½ c. homemade yogurt*, sweetened with honey (opt.)

*See page 7 for an explanation of what makes this ingredient legal for the Specific Carbohydrate Diet.

Preheat oven to 350°. Generously butter and flour with coconut flour 9 muffin cups (if possible, use a shiny rather than a dark pan and set muffin pan in another muffin pan or on a baking sheet to prevent burning). Place a circle of parchment in the bottom of each muffin cup. In a bowl with a mixer, beat butter and honey until thoroughly combined and light. Add eggs and beat until incorporated, stopping to scrape down inside of bowl. Add almond and coconut flours, orange zest, vanilla, and salt and beat on low speed to combine.

Divide batter among prepared muffin cups. Poke 1 grape into batter in each cup. Cut remaining grapes in half lengthwise; set 2 halves on batter in each cup. Sprinkle with sliced almonds.

Bake until deep golden brown, 20 to 22 minutes, turning pan halfway through. Let cool in pan on a rack at least 15 minutes. Loosen and remove cakes from pan with a knife, remove parchment circles. Set on small plates, and serve with a spoonful of sweetened yogurt if you like.

Banana Ice Cream

We made tiny scoops of this frozen yogurt ice cream with a melon ball maker for the kids' Pirate Party on NoMoreCrohns. We combined them with scoops of Crushed Cherry Frozen Yogurt, p. 147 in cantaloupe "boats" and decorated them with pirate flags! It was a nice birthday cake alternative! Scoop a day or two in advance and freeze balls in paper lined muffin cups so they'll be ready when you need them.

¾ c. honey
3 eggs
4 Tbs. butter*
3 medium speckled bananas*
2 Tbs. lemon juice
2 c. homemade yogurt*
3 tsp. vanilla*

In a saucepan over medium-low heat, constantly whisk the honey, eggs, and butter together until thick and starting to boil. Allow to cool for an hour.

Cut bananas into a food processor and add the lemon juice. Process until pureed, or, alternatively, push bananas through a strainer and stir in lemon juice.

Combine honey mixture, banana mixture, yogurt, and vanilla. Mix well with a whisk or electric mixer. Pour into a countertop electric ice cream maker and process for about a half hour, or until thick and creamy. Pour into a freezer container with a lid and freeze immediately until firm.

*See page 7 for an explanation of what makes this ingredient legal for the Specific Carbohydrate Diet.

Coconut Vanilla Ice Cream

One of Erin's favorites, she makes this ice cream often!

- 2 cans full fat coconut milk*
- 10 Medjool dates, seeded and cut into a few pieces
- 1/3 c. honey
- 2 Tbs. vanilla*

Blend all ingredients in a blender or food processor until well blended. Transfer to a countertop ice cream maker and churn until thick, about a half hour. Spoon into a freezer container and freeze until firm.

Pumpkin Ice Cream

This is very gourmet tasting ice cream!

- 2 c. homemade yogurt*
- 1 c. canned* or fresh pumpkin puree
- ½ c. honey
- 2 tsp. cinnamon
- 1 tsp. nutmeg
- ½ tsp. cloves

Place all ingredients in a blender and process until smooth. Pour into a counter-top electric ice cream maker and mix for about 30 minutes, or until thick and creamy. Spoon into a freezer container and freeze until firm.

Vanilla Ice Cream

Try this with peanut butter* and peanuts on top, or strawberries and chopped pecans or Apple Pie Treat, p. 150! Or put a scoop on your piece of Butternut Pecan Pie, p. 132. Yum! The eggs in this recipe give it extra richness.

¾ - 1 c. honey (to taste)
4 Tbs. butter*
3 eggs
2½ c. homemade yogurt*
3 tsp. vanilla*

In a saucepan over medium-**low** heat, constantly whisk the honey, butter, and eggs together to keep the eggs from scrambling, until thick and starting to boil. Allow to cool (using the freezer will cool it faster).

Combine yogurt, and vanilla, and add to the honey-egg mixture. Mix well using a whisk or electric mixer.

Pour into a countertop electric ice cream maker, and process for about a half hour; or until thick and creamy. Spoon into a freezer container and freeze immediately until firm.

*See page 7 for an explanation of what makes this ingredient legal for the Specific Carbohydrate Diet.

Cantaloupe Frozen Yogurt

The season for juicy sweet cantaloupe runs all summer long. If the fruit is not quite ripe when purchased, store it at room temperature to allow it to ripen. When we were kids our Grandpa used to give us scoops of vanilla ice cream in bowls made with half a cantaloupe, and this frozen yogurt combines all the best flavors of that great dessert. You could make strawberry frozen yogurt by substituting 3 cups pureed strawberries, or peach frozen yogurt with 3 cups ripe peaches. So many possibilities!

- 1 sweet cantaloupe, pureed (about 3 c.)
- ¾ c. honey
- ½ envelope unflavored gelatin (about 1 tsp.)
- 2 Tbs. unsweetened additive free white grape juice or apple cider*
- 2 c. homemade yogurt*

Combine fruit puree and honey and allow mixture to rest on the kitchen counter for one to two hours so flavors can ripen.

Sprinkle gelatin on juice to soften for 3-4 minutes. Heat, stirring, just until gelatin dissolves. Set aside.

Place fruit mixture, gelatin mixture, and yogurt in an ice cream maker and freeze according to the manufacturers directions. Pack into a freezer container and place in your refrigerator's freezer for a few hours to further firm up until scooping consistency.

Strawberry Orange Ice in Orange Halves

Makes 8 servings

Light and refreshing, these little individual fruit ices are filled with delicious fruit flavor; they're fun to make ahead and have ready in the freezer to serve as a snack or simple dessert.

**4 medium oranges
3 c. whole strawberries or 3 c. frozen sliced unsweetened strawberries, partially thawed
2/3 c. honey**

Halve and ream the juice from oranges, saving orange shells. Whirl strawberries in a food processor to make 2 cups of puree. Measure orange juice and add a little **water** if necessary to make 1½ cups. Thoroughly combine orange juice, honey, and strawberry puree; cover and freeze until solid.

Meanwhile, using one of your sharper spoons, remove pulp from orange shells by starting at the cut edge and working into the center making sure not to make a hole (but if you do, you can plug it with some pulp). Stack and wrap shells, keeping their shape, and freeze.

Remove fruit-ice from freezer and let stand until you can break it into pieces with a dinner knife. Pour into a large mixing bowl and continue to smash ice into smaller pieces. With an electric mixer, beat slowly at first, then gradually at higher speeds until mixture is slushy; whip until smooth like a thick cake batter. Cover and almost completely refreeze.

Fill frozen orange halves with scoops of strawberry orange ice, place in muffin tins to keep upright; cover and return to freezer to harden until serving. If storing, put hardened ices in a zip-top bag to maintain flavor.

Crushed Cherry Frozen Yogurt

Photo credit: Pexels

Crushed Cherry Frozen Yogurt has great taste and texture! We served it at a children's party in little scoops made in advance with a melon baller and frozen in paper lined muffin cups. When processing the cherries, keep your eyes open for any cherry pits that may have escaped the pitting process. They turn up once in a great while.

½ envelope unflavored gelatin (about 1 tsp.)
2 Tbs. fresh orange juice
¾ c. honey
2/3 c. water
1¼ c. frozen pitted cherries
2¼ c. homemade yogurt*
3 tsp. vanilla*

*See page 7 for an explanation of what makes this ingredient legal for the Specific Carbohydrate Diet.

Sprinkle gelatin on orange juice to soften, and set aside.

Combine honey and water; heat gently, stirring, then bring to a boil and boil for 3 minutes. Reduce heat and add cherries. Bring to a boil again and let simmer for about 10 minutes, or until cherries are soft. Add a little of the hot liquid to the gelatin/juice mixture to dissolve gelatin. Cool cherry mixture.

When cherries are cold, put cherry syrup mixture in a food processor and process until coarsely chopped. Do not puree. If desired, after processing add 8-10 additional cherries, chopped, to make it more chunky. Stir in yogurt and vanilla and freeze in an ice cream freezer according to manufacturers directions for about 30 minutes or until frozen. Spoon into a freezer container and freeze for several hours before scooping.

Frosty Strawberries

Serves 9

> **1 packet unflavored gelatin powder (about 2 tsp.)**
> **½ c. apple cider***
> **1 package (16 oz.) frozen unsweetened strawberries thawed**
> **2 c. homemade yogurt***
> **½ c. honey (or more to taste)**
> **1 tsp. vanilla***
> **5 small limes, halved**
> **9 c. (72 oz.) club soda**

*See page 7 for an explanation of what makes this ingredient legal for the Specific Carbohydrate Diet.

In a small saucepan, sprinkle gelatin over apple cider and allow to soften for 3-5 minutes. Heat, stirring, until gelatin is completely dissolved. Set aside.

In a large bowl, mash strawberries with a fork. Stir in yogurt, honey and vanilla. Stir gelatin mixture into strawberry mixture. Transfer to a freezer-proof container. Cover and freeze for 4 hours or longer, until firm. Remove from the freezer 15 minutes before serving. To serve, scoop ½ cup frozen mixture into a glass; squeeze juice of one half lime over strawberry mixture; fill with 1 cup club soda (or you may use lemon-lime soda for non-SCDers).

Photo credit: Pexels

Watermelon Jello Dessert

Serves 6

This is a fresh grown-up dessert, adapted from Sunset Magazine. It's a light, tasty, and fruity finish to a summer meal, and would also make a sweet finale at an afternoon tea, chilled in pretty tea cups instead of dishes!

- **3 envelopes unflavored gelatin (about 6 tsp.)**
- 2/3 c. honey
- **4 c. watermelon juice (from 8 lb. watermelon, directions follow)**
- **watermelon balls**
- **1 c. homemade yogurt***
- **2-3 Tbs. honey (or to taste)**
- **¼ c. thinly sliced mint leaves**

Place yogurt in a coffee filter-lined strainer and allow it to drip while you make and chill the watermelon mixture.

Make 18 watermelon balls with a melon baller, to garnish 6 servings; set aside. Cut up watermelon and put chunks in the food processor. Puree, then strain into a large saucepan or bowl with a pouring spout to get 4 cups of juice.

Sprinkle gelatin over 1 c. **cold water** in a small saucepan and let stand 1 minute. Heat until mixture is hot and gelatin is melted. Add 2/3 c. honey, whisking until dissolved. Whisk gelatin mixture into watermelon juice. Divide mixture between 6 glass dishes (about 8 oz. each). Chill until set, about 2 hours.

Stir 2-3 Tbs. honey into thickened yogurt. Top each serving with three melon balls, a dollop of the honey-sweetened yogurt, and a sprinkle of sliced mint leaves.

Apple Pie Treat

Serves 2

Enjoy this fruity treat for breakfast, lunch, dinner, or snack! It would taste delicious as a side dish with pork tenderloin, or put it over yogurt and sprinkle it with nuts. It's easy comfort food that really hits the spot. Photo shows a generous double batch.

- **2 apples, peeled and sliced**
- **2 Tbs. butter***
- **3 Tbs. honey**
- **½ tsp. cinnamon**
- **¼ c. chopped walnuts (opt. to sprinkle on top)**

Place apples in a saucepan, then add butter, honey, and cinnamon. Cook, stirring occasionally, until apples are tender, 10-12 minutes. Sprinkle with nuts if desired.

Photo credit: PNG Mart

Real Deal Coconut Macaroons

Makes 16-20 macaroons

My great-aunt and uncle used to love to drive into Los Angeles and go to Clifton's Cafeteria for lunch. They would often bring home a pink box filled with moist and chewy macaroons as a treat for us, and we loved them! I call these "Real Deal" macaroons because they are so much like those wonderful cookies that I remember! I hope you try them, but you should wait until your symptoms have significantly cleared up before eating these yummy coconut cookies.

3 c. unsweetened shredded coconut
¾ c. honey
¾ c. egg whites (from about 5 large eggs)
1½ tsp. vanilla*

Place the coconut, honey, and egg whites in a heavy 2- to 3-quart saucepan and stir well. Cook over medium-low heat, stirring almost continuously, 10 to 15 minutes. The mixture will look creamy as it heats, and then it will slowly get a bit drier, with flakes of coconut becoming more obvious.

Stop cooking when it no longer looks creamy but is still quite sticky and moist, not dry. Remove from heat and stir in vanilla. Scrape mixture onto a small baking sheet, spread it out to cool quickly, and refrigerate until cold, 30 minutes.

Preheat oven to 300°. Line a baking sheet with parchment paper.

Firmly form coconut mixture into balls the size of a golf ball. Space them evenly on the prepared baking sheet.

Bake the macaroons until golden, about 30 minutes, turning pan once half way through. Cool completely on the pan on a wire rack. Transfer them to an airtight container and refrigerate for up to 5 days or freeze.

*See page 7 for an explanation of what makes this ingredient legal for the Specific Carbohydrate Diet.

Cookie Press Cookies

Makes about 8 dozen

You will love this great recipe adapted from pecanbread.com. It makes delicious Christmas cookies for everyone… so make plenty! We divided the dough in half and added cooked beet pulp for color to one half and orange zest to the other half. A drop or two of pure peppermint oil could be added to the beet portion for a wonderful winter time flavor and look. Ghee is the pure oil separated from the milk solids in butter and can be purchased at Indian or International grocery stores and at Aldi. Look online for instructions on how to make your own ghee at home.

6½ to 7 c. almond flour
1 tsp. baking soda
1 c. ghee
1 c. honey
1 egg
1 tsp. vanilla*

*See page 7 for an explanation of what makes this ingredient legal for the Specific Carbohydrate Diet.

Additions, if desired:

1 Tbs. beet pulp (Cook a piece of fresh beet then mash thoroughly with a fork or press through a strainer.)
½ tsp. orange zest

Combine almond flour and baking soda, pinching out lumps; set aside.

In a large bowl, combine ghee, honey, egg, and vanilla and beat several minutes until very light and fluffy. Beat in flour mixture until it is very stiff, like dough that you could roll out. If making different flavors, at this point remove half of your dough to a second bowl. Add beet pulp to one bowl, plus a little almond flour to bring dough back to the right consistency. Add orange peel to the second bowl. Beat thoroughly.

Preheat oven to 350°. Put cookie dough in cookie press and press out desired shapes onto greased cookie sheets. Bake cookies for 8 to 10 minutes. Watch carefully so they don't get too brown. Cookies with beet added may need the full 10 minutes to fully bake through, and make a slightly more chewy cookie.

Peanut Butter Cookies

Serves 6

Erin says, "Remembering the delicious peanut butter cookies from my childhood that my mom made for parties, camping trips, holidays… or just because, I set out to make one that measured up. This one definitely hits the spot and I think it will for you too!"

- 1½ c. almond flour
- ¼ c. coconut flour
- 2 tsp. baking soda
- ¼ tsp. salt
- 1 egg
- 2 tsp. vanilla*
- 2/3 c. peanut butter*
- 2/3 c. honey
- 3/4 c. chopped unsalted peanuts

Note: A tip for crispier cookies: Cool oven to 170° and re-bake cookies for 1.5 to 2 hours. It really gives you a satisfying crunch!

Stir dry ingredients together in a large bowl. Add wet ingredients and mix together. Because the dough is so sticky, stir by hand if needed, using a strong rubber spatula. Add peanuts and stir well. Roll dough in balls and place on cookie sheets lined with parchment. Use a fork to make a criss-cross design. Clean the fork in a bowl of water between every one or two cookies to prevent sticking. Bake at 320°F for 10-12 minutes, until edges are golden brown.

Artwork credit: Pixabay

Peanut Butter Cookie Bars

Makes 16 bars

Try these wonderful bar cookies adapted from Breaking the Vicious Cycle. They make great take-alongs when you head out on the road or have a picnic. Make some today.

> 1¼ c. chunky peanut butter*
> ½ c. honey
> 1 egg
> 1 tsp. vanilla*
> ½ tsp. baking soda

Combine ingredients and pour into a buttered 8" x 8" which has been lined with a piece of parchment. Bake at 300° for 30 minutes.

*See page 7 for an explanation of what makes this ingredient legal for the Specific Carbohydrate Diet.

Pork Rind Krispy Treats

Makes 12-16 treats

A great recipe from Gay Bauer, founder of the SCD website scd.net, that can really fill your Rice Krispy Treat cravings!

- **1 pkg. plain pork rinds with salt only**
- **1 c. honey**
- **1 egg white**
- **1 tsp. vanilla***
- **¼ c. salted butter***

Snip a small hole at the top of the pork rind bag to let the air out. Smash the pork rinds with a rolling pin. Pour into a large mixing bowl and set aside. (Erin warns you that her kids told her the pork rinds don't smell very great at this point, but look past that and keep going! They're going to taste great and lose that odor soon!)

Butter an 8x8 baking dish and set aside. Beat the egg white in a small bowl until frothy; set aside.

Boil the honey over medium heat for 7-10 minutes, until a small amount dropped into cold water forms a hard ball or until it reaches 124°F. on a candy thermometer (warning - don't let the honey boil over!). Remove from heat. Add butter.

Gradually add the honey mixture to the egg white, mixing well. Add vanilla slowly. Whip until stiff. Stir honey mixture into the pork rinds and stir well. Spread evenly in your prepared baking dish and cool. Cut into squares and enjoy!

Refrigerate leftovers, covered, or freeze in a zip-top bag for later.

Baked Raspberry Custard

Serves 6

Good in any season, feel free to substitute other soft fruit, like speckled bananas, pitted cherries or ripe pears for the raspberries in this recipe adapted from Everyday Food Magazine. Make this quick and delicious "winner" tonight!

Photo credit: Pexels

- ¼ c. butter*, unsalted
- ¾ c homemade yogurt*
- 3 large eggs, at room temperature
- ½ c. honey
- ¼ c. coconut flour
- ¼ tsp. coarse salt
- ½ tsp. vanilla*
- 2 c. raspberries (about 9 oz.)

Preheat oven to 375°. In oven, melt butter in a 9-inch pie plate, about 6 minutes.

In a blender, combine yogurt, eggs, honey, coconut flour, salt, and vanilla; blend mixture until smooth, 30 seconds.

Distribute berries (or other soft fruit) evenly in pie plate and pour batter over top. Bake until slightly puffed and set in the middle, 25-28 minutes. Serve warm or at room temperature.

"When it comes to food, taking the time to make and eat meals is an act of deep self-care. It is a celebration. It is a simple, significant approach to create warmth, memories, and magic."

Stephanie Pedersen, "American Cozy"

Panna Cotta with Raspberries

Serves 6

Recipe is inspired by one in Saveur Magazine.

For the Panna Cotta:
  2½ c. homemade yogurt*, drained for 1
    hour in a coffee filter lined sieve
  1½ t. unflavored gelatin
  ¾ c. honey
  2 tsp. vanilla*

For the Raspberry Puree:
  4 c. fresh or thawed frozen raspberries
  ¾ c. honey

  6 c. mixed fresh berries
  honey for drizzling

For the panna cotta: Remove ¼ c. yogurt to a small saucepan and heat over medium heat until just hot. Remove from heat and stir in gelatin to dissolve it, 2-3 minutes.

Combine remaining dripped yogurt and honey and whisk to combine. Stir a half cup of this mixture into the gelatin mixture. Whisk yogurt-gelatin mixture back into yogurt-honey mixture.

Divide mixture evenly between six 3-inch wide ramekins (ramekins should be at least 1½ inches tall; we used custard cups). Transfer ramekins to a sheet pan, cover with plastic wrap, and refrigerate until completely set, 8 hours or overnight.

For the raspberry puree: Put raspberries and honey into a blender and puree, adding up to 2 Tbs. **water** if needed. Press puree through a fine sieve, discarding solids.

To serve: Pour one sixth of the raspberry puree onto the middles of 6 plates. Set each ramekin in a hot-water bath for 1-2 minutes, run a sharp knife around the edges, and turn panna cotta out onto the plates. Place 1 c. of berries around each panna cotta and drizzle berries with honey.

*See page 7 for an explanation of what makes this ingredient legal for the Specific Carbohydrate Diet.

Food With Friends

Bread Pudding

Serves 6-8

Recipe is provided by Gay Bauer, SCD veteran! Erin says, when chilled, it tastes like cheesecake.

3 c. almond flour
¼ c. melted butter*
½ c. raisins
1 tsp. cinnamon

6 eggs
½ c. honey
2 tsp. vanilla*
¼ tsp. salt
3 c. homemade yogurt*

For Butter Sauce
½ c. *each;* **honey and water**
½ Tbs. almond flour
2 Tbs. butter*
1 tsp. vanilla*

*See page 7 for an explanation of what makes this ingredient legal for the Specific Carbohydrate Diet.

Place yogurt between two thick stacks of paper towels for 5 to 10 minutes. Scrape off with a rubber spatula and use as directed.

Meanwhile, preheat oven to 375°. Combine almond flour, butter, raisins, and cinnamon and mix well. Spread flour mixture evenly in the bottom of a well-buttered 9x13-inch glass baking dish.

In a bowl, mix together eggs, honey, vanilla, salt, and thickened yogurt until smooth. Pour over almond flour mixture in the baking dish. Let it soak in for five minutes. Sprinkle with nutmeg and bake for around 35 minutes, until egg mixture on top is well cooked and firm.

While bread pudding bakes, make Butter Sauce to pour on when the pudding is done. Mix all sauce ingredients in a small saucepan. Cook until it thickens, about 15 minutes at medium heat. Pour over pudding after it has cooled. Store pudding in the refrigerator.

English Toffee Candy

Makes about ¾ pound candy

- ½ c. finely chopped unsalted nuts (peanuts, cashews, pecans, or almonds)
- ½ c. butter*
- ½ c. honey
- 3 Tbs. ground almonds or other nuts (or almond flour)

Generously butter a shallow 8 x 8-inch microwave safe baking dish. Sprinkle nuts evenly on bottom.

In a saucepan, melt butter over medium heat. Gradually add honey, stirring to combine. Cook over medium heat, stirring occasionally to prevent burning, 7 to 9 minutes, or until mixture turns a deep golden brown, but before it burns.

Pour over nuts in pan, sprinkle with ground nuts and cool slightly. If candy does not get really hard, put candy into the microwave for one-minute intervals until it is a deeper brown all over. With a knife, mark into 1-inch squares. Cool completely, chill if necessary, and break into pieces along lines.

Background credit: FreePik

Nut Butter Fudge

Makes 14-16

Inspired by a recipe from chocolatecoveredkatie, these sweet little morsels are quick and delicious! Using peanut butter and cocoa butter for the oil makes it feel like a Reese's Peanut Butter Cup! Serve and keep cold.

    ½ c. almond or other nut butter*
    2½ Tbs. food grade cocoa butter or coconut oil
    1½ Tbs. honey, or to taste

    Items to stir in and/or garnish, if desired:
        Unsweetened coconut
        Chopped raw pecans
        Chopped raw peanuts
        Sliced almonds
        ¼ tsp. vanilla *or* **dash cayenne pepper** *or* **dash cinnamon**

*See page 7 for an explanation of what makes this ingredient legal for the Specific Carbohydrate Diet.

Gently warm nut butter, oil, honey, and any additives. Fill a mini muffin pan with mini muffin paper liners. Fill each liner with one tablespoon fudge mixture. Chill 15-20 minutes, then sprinkle on toppings. Freeze a few hours; store in the refrigerator and serve cold.

Sugar Plums

Makes about 35 walnut sized sugar plums

"…while visions of sugarplums danced in their heads." The famous sugar plums spoken about in Clement Clark Moore's beloved poem, "Twas the Night Before Christmas," are made of spices and dried fruit. This recipe is taken from Saveur Magazine. The only change is that they are rolled in ground almonds or chopped unsweetened coconut instead of powdered sugar. They can be refrigerated between sheets of waxed paper in airtight containers for up to one month. Their flavor improves after ripening for several days.

- **2 c. whole raw almonds**
- **¼ c. honey (or more to taste)**
- **2 tsp. grated orange zest**
- **1½ tsp. ground cinnamon**
- **½ tsp. ground allspice**
- **½ tsp. nutmeg**
- **1 c. finely chopped dried apricots**
- **1 c. finely chopped pitted dates**
- **Almond flour or unsweetened coconut**

Preheat oven to 400°. Arrange almonds on a baking sheet in a single player and toast in oven for 10 minutes. Set aside to cool, then finely chop. Finely chop dried apricots and pitted dates as well. (We did this in batches in a food processor, but it may also be done by hand.)

Meanwhile, combine honey, orange zest, cinnamon, allspice, and nutmeg in a medium mixing bowl. Add almonds, apricots, and dates and mix well.

Pinch off rounded teaspoon-size pieces of the mixture and roll into balls. (Rinse hands as needed, as mixture is sticky.) Roll balls in ground almonds (almond flour) or chopped unsweetened coconut, then refrigerate in single layers between sheets of waxed paper in airtight containers for up to 1 month.

Background credit: FreePik

Salsas, Dips, & Sauces

Fresh Cranberry Salsa, 164

Heidi's Tomatillo Salsa, 164

Mama Grace's Green Salsa, 165

Triple Berry Salsa, 166

Pineapple Cranberry Salsa, 167

Chunky Guacamole, 168

Layered Taco Dip, 169

Hot Artichoke Dip, 170

Mimi's Spinach Artichoke Dip, 171

Navy Bean Hummus, 172

Salted Caramel Dip, 173

Basil Pesto, 174

Olive Tapenade, 175

Avocado Oil Mayonnaise, 176

Vinaigrette Salad Dressing, 177

Moroccan Spice Mix, 177

Food With Friends

Fresh Cranberry Salsa

Makes about 1 cup

Yummy with chicken, turkey, or shrimp, use up your leftover cranberries in the freezer and give this salsa, adapted from Coastal Living Magazine, a try. It's so good!

1½ c. fresh or frozen cranberries, thawed
3 Tbs. honey
½ tsp. lime zest
1 Tbs. fresh lime juice
1 green onion, thinly sliced
4 Tbs. chopped fresh cilantro
1 jalapeno pepper, seeded and minced (wear gloves)
1/8 tsp. ground cumin
1/8 tsp. salt

Pulse cranberries in a food processor 4 to 5 times or until coarsely chopped. Transfer to a medium bowl; stir in honey and remaining ingredients. Allow flavors to blend for a few minutes.

We served our salsa on chicken tenders browned in oil and sprinkled with a little cumin and salt.

Heidi's Tomatillo Salsa

Makes about 3 cups

My daughter, Heidi, created this salsa and makes it often. For more heat, leave the seeds and membranes in the peppers.

4 Anaheim or 2-3 Poblano peppers, roasted
  and peeled, instructions p. 62
7-10 tomatillos, papery outer layer removed, halved and broiled
  for about 5 minutes, or until skins are beginning to char
1 to 3 jalapenos, optional for additional heat, broiled
1 bunch cilantro, main stems cut off
juice of 1 lime (2-3 Tbs.)
1 tsp. salt + more to taste, if needed

Roast peppers, p. 62, peel, remove seeds and membranes, and place in a blender along with broiled tomatillos, including juices. Combine all ingredients in blender and blend until smooth, stirring down if needed. Refrigerate for up to 3 days. Great on eggs and with any Mexican food.

Mama Grace's Green Salsa

6-7 medium sized tomatillos, papery outer layer removed
1 c. water
1 tsp. salt
1 jalapeno pepper, seeds and ribs removed
1 serrano pepper, seeds and ribs removed
1 garlic clove, peeled and sliced
2 green onions, very finely chopped
8 or 9 stalks of cilantro plus a few more
1 or 2 slices of fresh tomato for garnish, if desired

Wash tomatillos and cut into chunks. Place in a saucepan with water and salt and bring to a boil, cooking for about five minutes. Cut up chile peppers (wear gloves) and add them to the saucepan, cooking for another 2 to 3 minutes. Remove from heat, add sliced garlic clove and allow to cool.

Pour tomatillo mixture into a blender along with a few cilantro sprigs and blend until fairly smooth. Gather remaining cilantro into a bouquet, holding it by the stems. Using a knife, cut and scrape off the top section of leaves, discarding stems. Roll cilantro leaves into a ball and finely slice. Combine chopped green onions and cilantro with blended salsa, pour into a serving bowl and garnish with a few pieces of finely diced red tomato. Serve with dippers such as unflavored fried pork rinds, cheese lace, p. 25, and vegetables.

Mama Grace with her daughter, Mina, enjoy her salsa with homemade guacamole.

See page 7 for an explanation of what makes this ingredient legal for the Specific Carbohydrate Diet.

Triple Berry Salsa

Makes about 5 cups of salsa

This beautiful salsa from Healthy Cooking Magazine is a fresh, flavorful blend of healthy berries and veggies and tastes refreshing over grilled chicken or fish.

1½ c. fresh blueberries
¾ c. fresh strawberries, chopped
¾ c. fresh raspberries
1 medium tomato, seeded and chopped
1 small yellow or orange bell pepper, chopped
¼ c. finely chopped red onion
¼ c. minced fresh cilantro
1 jalapeno pepper, seeded and minced (wear gloves)
2 green onions, chopped

1 Tbs. cider vinegar
1 Tbs. olive oil
2 tsp. fresh lime juice
2 tsp. fresh orange juice
1 tsp. honey
¼ tsp. salt

In a large bowl, combine the first nine ingredients. In a small bowl, whisk the remaining ingredients. Drizzle over salsa; toss to coat. Chill until serving. Serve with veggie dippers or over cooked meats.

Pineapple Cranberry Salsa

Makes 3 cups

Pink and refreshing, this salsa from Light & Tasty features cranberries, pineapple, strawberries, and a sprinkling of cilantro. Pull it together to jazz up chicken or pork.

- **1 c. fresh or frozen cranberries**
- **1/3 c. water**
- **1/3 c. honey**
- **2 c. fresh pineapple, cut into small bits**
- **1 c. coarsely chopped fresh or frozen strawberries**
- **1 jalapeno pepper, seeded and finely chopped (wear gloves)**
- **2 Tbs. lime juice**
- **2 Tbs. minced fresh cilantro**
- **1/8 tsp. salt**

In a small saucepan, combine the cranberries, water, and honey. Cook and stir over medium heat until the berries pop, about 15 minutes. Cool.

Transfer to a bowl; stir in the remaining ingredients. Store in the refrigerator.

Photo credit: PNG Mart

Chunky Guacamole

Fills 6 avocado halves

Jimmy Shaw, owner of Loteria Grill in Hollywood, created this excellent chunky guacamole and we found it in Los Angeles Magazine. For fun, create individual servings by filling the avocado skins with guacamole.

- 1½ to 2 whole onions, finely chopped
- 2-3 Serrano chiles, finely chopped (wear gloves)
- 3/4 c. tomato, finely chopped
- 3 Tbs. cilantro, roughly chopped
- salt to taste
- fresh lime juice to taste
- 3 large avocadoes, preferably Haas

*See page 7 for an explanation of what makes this ingredient legal for the Specific Carbohydrate Diet.

Combine onions, chiles, tomato, and cilantro in a bowl with salt and lime juice. Cut avocadoes in half and spoon pulp into a separate bowl. Use a fork to mash avocado, being sure to leave some texture.

Fold most of the onion mixture into the avocadoes, being careful to preserve texture of tomatoes and avocadoes. Garnish guacamole and serving plate with remaining onion mixture. Serve immediately at room temperature with veggie dippers.

Layered Taco Dip

Makes one large or two small serving platters

Who doesn't love layered taco dip for a party or as a fun main course?

- 2 c. cooked navy beans*, mashed
- about 2 c. cooked taco meat (¼ recipe, right)
- 2 Anaheim chiles, roasted and chopped*, p. 62
- 3 c. homemade yogurt*, dripped overnight, p. 10
- 1½ tsp. *each;* cumin and paprika
- 1½ tsp. salt, divided
- 2 tomatoes, diced
- 1 bunch green onions, chopped
- 1 bunch cilantro, stems removed, chopped
- juice of one lime (2-3 Tbs.)
- 1/8 tsp. hot pepper sauce*, or to taste
- 1 green or red bell pepper, diced
- 3 c. iceberg lettuce, shredded
- 2 c. freshly grated Cheddar or Monterey Jack cheese*
- 1 (6 oz.) can sliced black olives*, drained

Taco Meat

Recipe makes 4 pounds of meat, providing extra for future meals.

- 4 lb. ground beef
- 2 large onions, chopped
- 2 to 3 jalapenos, finely diced (wear gloves)
- 4 tsp. cumin
- 4 tsp. paprika
- 2 tsp. salt, to taste
- 3 tsp. dried oregano

In a large skillet, cook meat, onions and peppers until meat is no longer pink. Drain. Add cumin, paprika, salt, and oregano and stir to combine. Cool. Freeze in 4 individual qt. size zip-top freezer bags, labeled and pressed flat.

In a medium bowl, combine the warmed mashed beans, taco meat, diced green chiles, and ½ tsp. salt. Spread the mixture onto one large or two smaller serving platters.

Using a rubber spatula, combine yogurt, cumin, paprika, and 1 tsp. salt. Spread over the bean and meat mixture.

Combine diced tomatoes, green onions, cilantro, lime juice, and hot sauce. Spread over yogurt mixture. Top with bell pepper, lettuce, cheese, and olives. Serve with dippers such as diagonally cut cucumbers or Cheese Lace, p. 25.

Food With Friends

Hot Artichoke Dip

Be sure to get some of this creamy rich dip before it disappears completely! It's delicious.

1 bag frozen artichoke hearts, (about 3½ cups)
¾ c. homemade mayonnaise*, p. 176
5 oz. widely shredded Parmesan cheese* (about 1½ c.)
4-5 cloves garlic, chopped

*See page 7 for an explanation of what makes this ingredient legal for the Specific Carbohydrate Diet.

Preheat oven to 350°.

Place artichoke hearts in a medium saucepan and cover with water. Bring to a boil and simmer 8 minutes. Drain thoroughly and roughly chop.

Combine artichokes, mayonnaise, Parmesan cheese, and garlic. Place in an ovenproof serving dish and bake for 20 minutes, or until cheese is melted and dip is bubbly. Serve warm with veggies for dipping.

Note: A naturally occurring and safe chemical reaction may turn the garlic green.

Mimi's Spinach Artichoke Dip

This cheesy, rich dip is wonderful! It's perfect with veggies for dipping. The recipe, shared by Mimi's Café online, was adapted slightly and we're sure you'll love it.

4 oz. Jack cheese* (1 generous c. lightly pressed down)
2 oz. Swiss cheese* (about ½ c. lightly pressed down)
8 oz. freshly grated Parmesan cheese* (about 2½ c.)
1 c. frozen artichoke hearts, simmered for 10 minutes and drained
2 large handfuls fresh spinach
1 c. homemade mayonnaise*, p. 176
2 tsp. chopped garlic
½ tsp. black pepper
12 sun-dried tomato halves, soaked in boiling water for 15 minutes, drained

Note: This is the perfect recipe for a restaurant because they can make the cold mixture ahead and just heat each serving as it's ordered. You can do the same if people are eating in shifts! Photo shows the whole recipe.

Combine Jack, Swiss, and Parmesan cheeses in a large mixing bowl. Dice artichokes into small pieces. Wash and cut spinach into 1-inch pieces and add to cheese mixture.

In a small bowl combine the mayonnaise, garlic, and pepper. Mix until well combined. Pour mayonnaise mixture into the cheese mixture and stir until well mixed. Dice sun-dried tomatoes into small pieces and add to the cheese-mayonnaise mixture.

Heat cold dip mixture over medium heat in a non-stick skillet until hot, and cheese is completely melted. Transfer to serving dish and serve with veggies.

Navy Bean Hummus

1 2/3 c. dried white navy beans, picked over and soaked overnight
1 clove garlic, peeled
salt
½ c. tahini (sesame paste)
¼ c. fresh lemon juice
3 Tbs. extra-virgin olive oil
2 tsp. chopped parsley
¼ tsp. sweet paprika

Flavored Ground Beef

(Hummus ma Lahma)

¼ lb. lean ground beef
1/8 tsp. allspice
1/8 tsp. cinnamon
1/8 tsp. black pepper
salt to taste

Cook together until browned. Spoon into center of hummus.

Drain beans, discarding water, and transfer to a medium pot. Cover with water, and bring to a boil over medium-high heat. Reduce heat to medium-low and simmer, partially covered, until beans are tender and skins begin to crack, about 50 minutes. Drain well, reserving the cooking liquid, and set beans aside to let rest until cool enough to handle.

Remove obvious bean skins. Put beans and ¼ c. cooking liquid into a food processor and puree, occasionally scraping down bowl, until very smooth, 3-4 minutes. Transfer puree to a large bowl.

Put garlic and a pinch of salt into a mortar and crush with a pestle until they form a paste. Transfer garlic paste to bowl of pureed beans. Add tahini, lemon juice, and salt to taste and mix well to combine.

Transfer hummus to a shallow bowl and press a well into the center with the back of a spoon. Drizzle hummus with oil, sprinkle parsley and paprika into well, and top with a few whole beans, if you like. Serve with olives, vegetables, socca flatbread triangles, p. 44, and pita bread for non-SCDers.

The hummus in this picture is topped with delicious Flavored Ground Beef. See recipe in side bar.

Salted Caramel Dip

A recipe adapted slightly from Sprout's Farmer's Market.

1 c. dates, pitted
3 Tbs. honey
2 Tbs. almond butter*
dash of sea salt
2 Tbs. coconut oil, warmed slightly
1½ tsp. vanilla*

Soak dates in water for 1 hour, or longer if dates seem dry; drain. Combine all the ingredients in a food processor or blender, and blend until smooth and creamy, adding a little **almond milk* or water**, if needed, to facilitate blending.

Adjust flavors to taste and serve with sliced apples. Sprinkle with a pinch of kosher salt.

See page 7 for an explanation of what makes this ingredient legal for the Specific Carbohydrate Diet.

Food With Friends

Basil Pesto

Makes 1 cup

Pesto adds so much flavor to vegetables, scrambled eggs, fish, or chicken and can be added to homemade mayo*, p. 176, and used as a spread on meat sandwiches! We love it on pizza crusts, p. 42, topped with our favorite toppings. I'm sure you'll find many great uses for this pesto, adapted from simplyrecipes.

Note: Pesto made with all basil loses it's color quickly, so adding spinach or other green herbs helps maintain the bright green color and adds extra flavor.

1 c. fresh basil leaves, packed
1 c. baby spinach leaves, packed
1/3 c. walnuts
3 garlic cloves, minced (about 3 tsp.)
½ c. freshly grated Parmesan cheese*
½ c. olive oil
Salt and pepper to taste

Place the basil, spinach, and walnuts in a food processor and pulse several times. Add the garlic and Parmesan cheese and pulse several times more. Scrape down the sides of the food processor with a rubber spatula.

*See page 7 for an explanation of what makes this ingredient legal for the Specific Carbohydrate Diet.

While the food processor is running, slowly add the olive oil in a steady stream. Adding the olive oil slowly, while the processor is running, will help it emulsify and will help keep the pesto from separating. Occasionally stop to scrape down the sides of the food processor.

Add salt and pepper to taste. Refrigerate for up to a week, or freeze.

Olive Tapenade

Makes 1 cup

Adapted from Eat Well Live Well, this tapenade is delicious and makes a perfect salty sandwich filling, dip, or topping for soup. You could also fork it into a cooked half of a spaghetti squash with butter. Try working it into dripped yogurt "cheese" for a special dip! When I use Kalamata olives I like to double check that there are no pit fragments remaining.

> 1 c. brine-cured olives such as Kalamatas, pitted
> 2 cloves garlic, peeled and finely minced
> 1 Tbs. capers, drained
> 1½ Tbs. chopped fresh parsley
> 1 Tbs. grated lemon zest
> 2 Tbs. freshly squeezed lemon juice
> 2 Tbs. olive oil
> **Black pepper to taste**

In a food processor, process all the ingredients until finely chopped but not completely smooth. The tapenade can be stored in the refrigerator in a sealed container for up to 1 week.

Avocado Oil Mayonnaise

Adapted slightly from NourishedKitchen.com, this mayonnaise is mild tasting because of the avocado oil and best of all is foolproof! After many tries, Jenny McGruther hit on the successful idea of adding a little water to the egg yolks before adding any oil. This recipe makes about 2 cups of thick mayonnaise.

3 fresh egg yolks
½ tsp. coarse salt
1 Tbs. water
1 Tbs. fresh lemon juice
1 Tbs. vinegar
1½ c. very fresh avocado oil

Drop the egg yolks into the basin of a food processor, then sprinkle them with the salt. Add water, lemon juice, and vinegar. Pulse once or twice to combine, then turn it on so the blade continues moving.

Pour oil slowly into the feeder tube, allowing it to run into the egg yolk mixture in a very thin, smooth stream. Continue until all the oil is incorporated, about four minutes. Scrape mayonnaise into a jar with a tight fitting lid and store it in the refrigerator for up to a week.

Flexible Vinaigrette Salad Dressing

You can make this perfectly classic dressing or change it up with orange or lime juice instead of the vinegar. Make it creamy by adding a little tahini or homemade yogurt*, or add poppy seeds and additional honey for a sweeter dressing. For an Asian flair, use 2 Tbs. toasted sesame oil for part of the oil, orange juice instead of the vinegar, and remove the mustard.

- ½ c. olive oil (or other oil of your choice)
- 3 Tbs. apple cider vinegar* (or vinegar* of your choice)
- 1 Tbs. honey
- 1 Tbs. prepared yellow mustard*
- 2 medium cloves garlic, finely diced
- ¼ tsp. salt
- Freshly ground black pepper, to taste

Put ingredients in a jar with a tight fitting lid and shake it up. Taste, and adjust as necessary.

*See page 7 for an explanation of what makes this ingredient legal for the Specific Carbohydrate Diet.

How to Section a Grapefruit

With a sharp knife, slice off the ends of a grapefruit. Following the curve of the fruit, cut away peel and remaining white pith. Holding over a plate, cut out individual sections, reserving juice.

Moroccan Spice Mix

Combine and use as directed in various recipes or in the Mini Pork Brochettes recipe on page 112.

- 4 tsp. ground cinnamon
- 4 tsp. ground ginger
- 4 tsp. ground paprika
- 2 tsp. ground turmeric
- 2 tsp. ground pepper

Combine in a small labeled jar and use as directed.

Background credit: FreePik

Recipe Index

Appetizers & Snacks
- Amaretto Apricots, 17
- Bacon Wrapped Dates, 18
- Baked Brie with Winter Fruits, 23
- Carrot Curls, 19
- Cheese Balls, 22
- Cheese Lace Crackers, 25
- Front Porch Cheese Board, 26
- Fruit & Cheese Rolls, 24
- Party Poppers, 16
- Stuffed Mushrooms, 20
- Thai Chicken Satay, 21

Breads (also see Muffins)
- Apple Ginger Spice Scones, 36
- Best Banana Nut Bread, 38
- Cinnamon Rolls, 70
- Erin's Easy Sandwich Bread, 40
- English Muffins, 41
- Garlic Cheese Pizza Crust, 42
- Grain-Free Focaccia Bread, 81
- Nacho Cheese Triangles, 51
- Pizza Bread Rounds, 43
- Protein Bread, 39
- Rosemary Thyme Crackers, 50
- Socca Flatbread & Toppings, 44
- Socca Tortillas, Heidi's, 49

Cakes, Tarts, & Tortes
- Almond Torte with Fruit, 130
- Cocoa Butter Cakes, 139
- Fresh Orange & Yogurt Tart, 129
- Hummingbird Cake, 137
- Lemon Drizzle Cake, 138
- Mini Almond Grape Cakes, 141
- Nut Mosaic Tart, 128
- Peanut Butter Cake, 187
- Valentine Carrot Cakes, 186
- Western Fruitcake, 140

Candies
- English Toffee Candy, 159
- Nut Butter Fudge, 160
- Sugar Plums, 161

Recipe Index

Cookies
- Cinnamon Cookies, 185
- Coconut Almond Biscotti, 184
- Cookie Press Cookies, 152
- Fruit Cookies, 91
- Lemon Cookies, 185
- Peanut Butter Cookies, 153
- Peanut Butter Cookie Bars, 154
- Real Deal Coconut Macaroons, 151

Desserts
- Apple Pie Treat, 150
- Baked Raspberry Custard, 156
- Bread Pudding, 158
- Macaroon Squares & Toppings, 190
- Panna Cotta with Raspberries, 157
- Pork Rind Krispy Treats, 155

Dips
- Baked Onion Cheese Dip, 85
- Chunky Guacamole, 168
- Dipping Sauces for Chicken, 107
- Guacamole, 121
- Hot Artichoke Dip, 170
- Layered Taco Dip, 169
- Mimi's Spinach Artichoke Dip, 171
- Navy Bean Hummus, 172
- Salted Caramel Dip, 173
- Sun Dried Tomato Dip, 73
- Tzatziki Dip/Sauce, 72, 114

Drinks (Also see Smoothies)
- Cucumber Limeade, 28
- Ginger Pineapple Sparkling Punch, 29
- Strawberry Lemonade, 92

Frozen & Chilled Desserts
- Banana Ice Cream, 142
- Banana Raspberry Dessert, 191
- Cantaloupe Frozen Yogurt, 145
- Coconut Vanilla Ice Cream, 143
- Crushed Cherry Frozen Yogurt, 147
- Frosty Strawberries, 148
- Pumpkin Ice Cream, 143
- Strawberry Orange Ice in Orange Halves, 146
- Vanilla Ice Cream, 144
- Watermelon Jello Dessert, 149

Group Meals
- Afternoon Tea, 93
- Baked Potato & Spaghetti Squash Bar, 60
- Breakfast Board Bacon & Egg Quiches, 68
- Front Porch Cheese Board, 26
- Holiday Open House Trays, 72
- Pizza Making Party, 64
- Polynesian Pile On, 74
- Pork Pozole Soup Bar, 76
- Socca Flatbread & Toppings, 44
- Spaghetti & Meatball Bar, 78
- Taco Salad Bar, 82
- Tailgate Party, 84

Meats (Also Tapas & Appetizers)
- Chicken Skewers & Avo Sauce, 87
- Flavored Ground Beef, 172
- Green Pork Chili Verde, 86
- Make Ahead Mini-Meatballs, 80
- Oven Roasted Tri-Tip Roast, 73
- Rosemary Meatballs, 73
- Taco Meat, 170
- Terrific Chili, No Beans, 62

Muffins
- Blueberry Streusel Muffins, 55
- Lemon Poppyseed Muffins, 53
- Orange Spice Muffins with Buttercream Icing, 54
- Very Lemon Muffins, 52

Pies
- Almond Pie Crust, 129
- Angel Pecan Pie, 188
- Banana Cream Pie, 189
- Butternut Pecan Pie, 132
- Cheddar Cheese Pie Crust, 128
- Erin's Favorite Pumpkin Pie, 133
- Lemon Ice-Box Pie, 135
- Nut Crust, 134
- Raspberry Mousse Pie, 136
- Yogurt Berry Pie, 134
- Yogurt Apple Pie, 131

Salads (Also see Tapas Sides)
- Carrot Radish Salad, 89
- Fresh & Fruity Coleslaw, 88
- Kale, Apple, Orange & Pecan, 63

Salad Dressings
- Aunt Trish's Dressing, 79
- Cilantro Dressing, 83
- Coleslaw Dressing, 88
- Flexible Vinaigrette Dressing, 177
- Herbed Yogurt Ranch Dressing, 66

Sauces, Relishes, & Spreads
- Avocado Sauce, 87
- Baking Sauces for Chicken, 107
- Basil Pesto, 174
- Caramelized Onions, 47
- Chile Zucchini Topper, 46
- Easy Marinara Sauce, 67
- Honey Lemon Curd, 138
- Mayonnaise, Avocado Oil, 176
- Olive Relish, 45
- Olive Tapenade, 175
- Smoky Carrot Spread, 45
- Sweet-Spicy Cherries, 47
- Tomato Tapenade, 100

Salsas
- Flag Salsa, 60
- Fresh Cranberry Salsa, 164
- Heidi's Tomatillo Salsa, 164
- Mama Grace's Green Salsa, 165
- Pineapple Cranberry Salsa, 167
- Triple Berry Salsa, 166

Spice Mixes
- Curry Powder, 21 & 74
- Moroccan Spice Mix, 177
- Spice Rub, 73
- Taco Seasoning Mix, 76

Smoothies
- Autumn Pumpkin Smoothie, 32
- Frozen Fruit Smoothie, 33
- Strawberry Colada Smoothie, 31
- Vitamix Green Smoothie, 30

Tapas, Main Dish
- Asian Chicken Lettuce Wraps, 108
- Camembert Popovers, 100
- Chicken in Lemon & Garlic, 109
- Chicken & Olive Roll-Ups, 110
- Chicken Salad with Raisins, 105
- Chile Cheese Squares, 101
- Deviled Eggs, Ten Kinds, 102
- Falafel with Cucumber Salad, 114
- Mahimahi & Bacon Skewers, 99
- Mini Pork Brochettes, 112
- Oven Baked Tortilla, 103
- Paprika Spareribs, 112
- Porterhouse Steak with Garlic, 111
- Spanish Meatballs, 113
- Spinach Mushroom Tortilla, 104
- Tasty Chicken Wings, 106

Tapas, Side Dish
- Asparagus, Bacon & Almonds, 118
- Avocado Citrus Salad, 119
- Fattoush Country Salad, 119
- Figs with Blue Cheese, 120
- Garlic Mushrooms, 123
- Lima Beans with Bacon, 122
- Marinated Artichoke Hearts, 123
- Mexican Skillet Cakes, 121
- Seasoned Almonds, 118
- Zucchini Tabbouleh, 122

Miscellaneous
- Buttercream Icing, 54
- Candied Lemon Slices, 135
- Chicken Stock, 11
- Fruit Skewers, 90
- Homemade SCD Yogurt, 12
- How to Roast Chilies, 45, 62
- How to Section Grapefruit, 177
- Navy Beans, 13
- Spiced Pecans, 90
- Streusel Topping, 55

"There's nothing warmer than a welcome."
Stephanie Pederson in *"American Cozy"*

Background credit: FreePik

Italian Coconut Almond Biscotti

Makes 20-24 biscotti cookies

Enjoy dipping these deliciously dense Italian cookies in your tea!

- ½ c. honey
- ½ c. grapeseed oil
- 2 eggs
- 1 tsp. vanilla*
- 2 tsp. almond extract*
- 1 c. stirred coconut flour
- ½ c. stirred almond flour
- ¾ c. toasted slivered or sliced almonds

Preheat oven to 325°. Grease a baking sheet and place a piece of parchment paper on the sheet. Set aside.

Beat honey and oil together with an electric mixer until well blended, about 1 minute. Add eggs, one at a time, beating well after each addition. Beat in vanilla and almond extract.

Add half the coconut flour, then half the almond flour, beating until incorporated. Add final coconut flour and almond flour, beating until completely combined. Do not over beat.

With a rubber spatula, stir in slivered or sliced almonds. Using the spatula, plop the dough onto the cookie sheet in two long parallel logs, smoothing slightly on the sides and top. Bake for 18 to 20 minutes., or until brown, turning the tray once during baking for more even heat. Remove from the oven and cool slightly.

With a sharp knife, gently cut logs into 1-inch cookies, making about 10 or 12 per log. Gently tip biscotti onto their sides, spreading them evenly around the cookie sheet. Return pan to the oven for 12-15 minutes, or until cookies are a rich brown. Allow to cool. May be frozen.

Photo credit: Pixabay

See page 7 for an explanation of what makes this ingredient legal for the Specific Carbohydrate Diet.

Lemon Cookies

Makes 25 to 30

These delicious cookies are from Raman Prasad's cookbook, "Recipes for the Specific Carbohydrate Diet." They would be perfect for a tea or any special moment. The batter is delicious on its own, and can be enjoyed since it doesn't contain any eggs.

4 Tbs. butter*, melted
1/3 c. honey
1 tsp. lemon zest
1/8 tsp. baking soda
2¼ c. almond flour

Preheat oven to 350°. Grease a cookie sheet.

With a mixer, combine all ingredients in a bowl. Roll dough into small, ½-inch balls. Place balls on the greased cookie sheet, evenly spaced apart. Press down and flatten.

Bake until golden brown, 10 to 15 min. Allow to cool.

*See page 7 for an explanation of what makes this ingredient legal for the Specific Carbohydrate Diet.

Cinnamon Cookies

Makes 25 to 30

You'll love these pretty cookies from Lucy's SCD Cookbook!

4 Tbs. butter*, melted
1/3 c. honey
1 tsp. cinnamon
1/8 tsp. salt
¼ tsp. baking soda
2 c. almond flour
Pecan halves

Place butter in a mixing bowl. Add all other ingredients except pecans, stirring the flour in last. Form dough into 1-inch balls and place on a buttered cookie sheet. Press a pecan half into each ball to flatten it. Bake at 275°F for 10-15 minutes, or until done.

Valentine Carrot Cakes

Don't let Valentine's Day sneak up on you! Be ready with your own delicious treats using our favorite Carrot Cake recipe. Ice with our Buttercream Icing, page 54, colored with cherry juice.

3 c. almond flour
1 tsp. *each;* **salt, baking soda, nutmeg**
1 Tbs. cinnamon
5 eggs
½ c. honey
¼ c. grapeseed oil
3 c. carrots, grated
1 c. raisins
1 c. walnuts, chopped (opt.)

In a large bowl, combine almond flour, salt, baking soda, nutmeg, and cinnamon. In a separate bowl, with an electric mixer, combine eggs, honey, and oil. Stir carrots, raisins, and walnuts, if using, into wet ingredients. Stir wet ingredients into dry ingredients. Fill either heart shaped pans or cupcake liners ¾ full. Bake in a preheated 325° oven for 18-20 minutes, or until a toothpick inserted in the middle comes out clean.

Color Buttercream Icing, p. 54, pink by adding 1-2 Tbs. cooled juice from heated frozen cherries.

Photo credit: Pexels

Peanut Butter Cake

A favorite cake that is darling to look at and easy to make! Decorate it for a different occasion by topping it with mint leaves and pesticide-free edible flowers.

2 eggs
½ c. honey
1 tsp. vanilla*
½ tsp. baking soda
1¼ c. chunky peanut butter*

Preheat oven to 300°. Oil a pyrex baking dish or an 8-inch cake pan.

In a medium mixing bowl, beat together eggs, honey, vanilla, and baking soda until fluffy. Add peanut butter and mix until well blended. Mixture will be thick.

Transfer mixture to prepared pan and bake for 50-55 minutes, or until a skewer inserted in the center comes out clean. Cool for 20 to 25 minutes. Loosen cake by carefully pushing a flexible knife or spatula down the sides as far as you can; Using hot pads as needed, place flat serving plate on top of baking dish, holding the two together. Invert cake onto plate. Cool completely before frosting.

*See page 7 for an explanation of what makes this ingredient legal for the Specific Carbohydrate Diet.

Frosting

1 c. butter*, at room temperature
¾ c. honey
2 tsp. vanilla*
1 carrot, cooked until very soft, cooled and pureed
¼ c. peanut butter*

Mint leaves, optional, for decorations
Dried fruits and/or nuts, optional, for decorations
Carrot curls, carrot shavings, very thin slices of carrot, optional, for decorations

Note: You could make pink icing by cooking and pureeing a small beet instead of a carrot.

Cream butter until it starts to lighten. Add honey, vanilla, and pureed carrot and continue beating until fluffy. Add peanut butter, beating until smooth and light colored. Spread icing on cake and decorate as desired.

Angel Pecan Pie

Serves 6-8

Try this lovely dessert if you have some leftover egg whites floating around. Rich and delicious, make this sweet pie when you're planning to have company for dinner!

- **3 egg whites**
- **½ c. honey**
- **1 c. almond flour**
- **½ tsp. cinnamon**
- **¼ tsp. baking soda**
- **1 c. chopped pecans**

Preheat oven to 325°. In a dry frying pan over medium heat, stir-fry almond flour and cinnamon until mixture is toasted, about 8-10 minutes. Pour onto a plate to stop the cooking.

Beat the egg whites until almost stiff; when whites are beginning to stiffen, pour in honey in 3 batches, beating very well after each addition.

Combine cooled almond flour mixture, baking soda, and pecans in a mixing bowl and gently fold the egg whites into the mixture with a rubber spatula. Pour into a buttered 9-inch pie pan. Bake for 25-30 minutes, until lightly browned. Cool. Serve with honey-sweetened SCD yogurt, if you'd like.

Banana Cream Pie

Adapted from SCDRecipe.com, this pie is sweet, rich, and creamy.

Crust:
½ c. honey
1 egg
2 c. almond flour
2 tsp. vanilla*
½ mashed speckled banana

Mix all crust ingredients together and spread into a buttered pie dish. Bake for 20-25 minutes at 350° or until golden brown. Crust will partially flatten as it bakes. Set aside.

Filling:
¼ c. honey
1 egg
3 or 4 speckled bananas
½ tsp. vanilla*
1 tsp. lemon juice
pecan halves (opt.)

Mix all filling ingredients in a food processor until smooth and fluffy. Pour into a saucepan and cook over medium heat, stirring constantly, until thickened and bubbling. Pour into the crust and refrigerate for two hours or more before serving. Garnish with pecans if desired.

Macaroon Squares with Toppings

Serves 8

These macaroon squares can be refrigerated for up to 3 days. Top these dessert squares, adapted from Everyday Foods, with your favorite topping such as Crushed Cherry Frozen Yogurt, p. 147, or Honey Lemon Curd, p. 138. Wait to enjoy coconut until your symptoms are significantly improved.

> **8 c. unsweetened flaked coconut (from two 14-ounce bags)**
> **7 large egg whites**
> **½ c. honey**
> **¼ tsp. salt**
> **1½ tsp. vanilla***

Preheat oven to 350°. Oil an 8-inch square cake pan. Line pan with 2 pieces of parchment paper in both directions, leaving 2 inches overhanging on all sides. In a food processor, combine coconut, egg whites, honey, salt, and vanilla; process, scraping bowl as needed, until coconut is finely chopped, about 1 minute.

Transfer mixture to prepared pan, pressing firmly to evenly distribute; smooth top. Bake until top is deep golden brown, about 1 hour. Place pan on a rack; cool completely.

Invert pan and peel parchment from macaroons; cut off deep brown edges, then cut into 9 pieces. To serve, macaroon may be topped with honey-drizzled fruit of your choice, or see our suggestions, above and in the photo. We used the leftover egg yolks to make an "all yolk" lemon curd from the recipe on page 138.

*See page 7 for an explanation of what makes this ingredient legal for the Specific Carbohydrate Diet.

Frozen Banana Raspberry Dessert

Serves 12

This three-ingredient spring dessert can be made in a Bundt pan or shaped cake pan as well as a 9 x 13 pan. It is so tasty! You'll be surprised. It holds for quite a long time out of the freezer. The dessert in the picture had been on the plate for over an hour! The recipe can be easily cut in half and placed in a smaller pan.

- **32 oz. frozen raspberries**
- **2 c. almonds, slivered or roughly chopped**
- **10-12 speckled bananas**

Puree or thoroughly mash bananas and swirl raspberries into the puree.

Place half of the almonds on the bottom of a 9 x 13 pan or other pan of your choice. Top with banana raspberry mixture. Top with remaining nuts.

Cover with plastic wrap and freeze overnight. If making in a shaped pan, to serve, turn sideways and carefully run metal pan under hot water briefly, turning to warm all areas, until dessert loosens. Top with serving plate, then invert, allowing dessert to drop onto plate. Allow to soften about 20 minutes before cutting.

About The Author

From a young age Robin Cox was interested in cooking, and this passion developed over the years as she raised three daughters on delicious homemade meals, hosted church groups and foreign students, and directed the cooking for large events. When her daughter Erin was diagnosed with Crohn's Disease in 2001 and began the Specific Carbohydrate Diet, Robin tackled the challenge of making her delicious meals that were free of grains, lactose, and refined sugar. What at first seemed like a daunting task soon blossomed into many delicious possibilities under Robin's expert hand. Her love for foreign cultures and flavors, can-do attitude, and knowledge of what makes a great recipe combine to enrich the grain-free, lactose-free, gluten-free, and refined-sugar free community with more scope for the taste buds.

In 2007, Robin and Erin created NoMoreCrohns.com, a website containing a plethora of recipes, information, and experience they had gained over the years to spread the word about the SCD and help others be successful on the diet. Through meeting people on the SCD and understanding their need to enjoy food and continue living a fulfilling and interesting life, Robin was inspired to create this cookbook with ideas for gathering friends and sharing fun and delicious food, hoping it will inspire people to make their world a better place by connecting with others around the table.

Made in the USA
Coppell, TX
07 December 2019